Library of
Davidson College

THE SCOTTISH TONGUE

THE
SCOTTISH TONGUE

A Series of Lectures on the Vernacular Language of Lowland Scotland

Delivered to the Members of the Vernacular Circle
of the Burns Club of London.

By

W. A. CRAIGIE, M.A., LL.D.,
Professor of Anglo-Saxon, Oxford University.

JOHN BUCHAN, M.A., LL.D.

PETER GILES, M.A., LL.D.,
Master of Emmanuel, Cambridge University.

J. M. BULLOCH, M.A., LL.D.,
Editor of "The Graphic," Chairman, Vernacular Circle, Burns Club of London.

McGrath Publishing Company
College Park, Maryland

1970

427.9
C886s

Reprinted by
McGrath Publishing Co., 1970

ISBN: 0-8434-0119-2
LC # 72-119292

Reproduced from an original copy lent by the
University of North Carolina Library at Chapel Hill

Manufactured in the United States of America
by Arno Press Inc., New York

CONTENTS

LECTURE	PAGE
I. The Present State of the Scottish Tongue	1
II. Some Scottish Characteristics	47
III. Dialect in Literature	89
IV. The Delight of the Doric in the Diminutive	125

FOREWORD

THIS book is an outcome of the Vernacular Circle of the Burns Club of London; and the Circle itself is, in turn, the outcome—quite unconscious—of a stream of tendency, coming apparently from nowhere, but instinctively seeking to fertilise the rich pastures of old forms of language and dialect, which display an increasing resistance to various processes of standardisation.

The significance of the work of this particular Vernacular Circle, which concentrates on Lowland Scots, becomes all the greater in virtue of the fact that the contributions to the subject presented here are all the work of men, living furth of Scotland, who are immersed in busy life, and that none of them is doctrinaire, some of them indeed being non-professional students of language.

One and all of them, however, have had their attention arrested by the Anglicising of the Scottish Lowland language which has been affecting the speech of the people. This influence, which has been at work for many a year, has not been in any sense a propagandist movement inspired by England

Foreword

itself. It has been the result of several tendencies, some natural, but some quite unnatural.

To begin with, there has been an inclination of snobbish, though often illiterate, parents to discourage the Lowland Scots language as a mark of lowly birth, and consequently to be avoided. Then there has been an altogether erroneous but understandable idea that Scots boys are hampered in their lives out of Scotland by their native speech, and that therefore Lowland Scots must be banned. So far, however, from that being necessary, we are faced by the fact that the main support of the movement for fair-play for the Lowland language has been initiated by Scots in fairly responsible positions, living outside Scotland. The only opposition that has been offered to the movement has been by Scots living in Scotland, though they are the very people who would rise in rebellion were any open attempt made to Anglicise the institutions of their native land.

Having in view the danger ahead, the Burns Club of London in 1920 formed a Vernacular Circle to devise a method for preserving from entire destruction the lan-

Foreword

guage in which the mentality of the Lowland Scot can best be expressed.

The enthusiasm of earnest Scots men and women living out of Scotland was immediately guaranteed, and they sought to extend this enthusiasm to their native heath, for by the gifts of patriotic Scotsmen prizes were established in the four Scottish universities and in several of the parish schools.

The Lecture scheme was heartily encouraged by Scottish professors at English universities, and the illuminating lectures of Professor W. A. Craigie, Oxford; Professor Peter Giles, Cambridge; and Professor Gordon, Oxford, have helped to kill most of the unthinking criticism of the movement.

It has been impossible to find room in this volume for all the lectures delivered, but it is hoped that those by the Marquis of Aberdeen, Professor Gordon, and others may be included in a further volume.

The work started in London has now been taken up in Scotland, where a Vernacular Committee has been formed by the Burns Federation, under the presidency of Sir Robert Bruce. Thus the movement has entered a new and important phase; and,

Foreword

with the work being done in Scotland itself, greater progress must be expected. The full results of such a movement as this cannot be seen in this generation, but the pioneers who have helped to organise the whole trend of sense and sentiment inherent in the Circle feel that they are taking part in a great movement, which, if making for a fulfilment of our separate selves, is in no way inimical to the essential, if subtle, unity of our Commonwealth.

WILLIAM WILL,
Hon. Secretary, Vernacular Circle.

The Present State of the Scottish Tongue

By W. A. CRAIGIE, M.A., LL.D.
Professor of Anglo-Saxon, Oxford University.

Delivered at the Scots Corporation Hall, Crane Court, Fleet Street, London, on January 10, 1921.

I HAVE selected the subject of my discourse this evening—"The Present State of the Scottish Tongue"—in a spirit which I am afraid is not regarded as characteristically Scottish—in a spirit of some humility. This is one of the few things connected with the land beyond the Tweed of which the patriotic and reflective Scot has not full reason to be proud. If any one is inclined to be doubtful on that point, I shall use only one argument to support my own view. If the Scottish tongue were in that flourishing state in which we would like to see it, would I be standing here—in the midst of a gathering of Scots, and in the very centre of that foreign capital which they have all but made their own—and yet be addressing you (as far as I can) in the language of the Southron? This is not as it ought to be; and yet if I had attempted to frame my address throughout in the "haimert tongue," in the current speech of Forfarshire, it would not only have been a surprise, but perhaps something of a trial, to you. It would certainly have demanded much more preparation on my part, and even more indulgence on yours than I trust I may rely upon while I unfold my views on this important subject.

The reason why I do not address you in our own tongue, even when speaking about it, can only be clearly understood by going back beyond our own time. It is no fault of ours, nor even of our fathers or grandfathers, but of still earlier generations, which allowed the germs of decay to creep into the fabric of the old Scottish tongue as it had grown up in the centuries when Scotland was a kingdom. In the sixteenth century, and especially in the first half of it, Scottish as a spoken and written language stood on a level with English, and in some respects even stood higher. The first real blow to it came through the Reformation. Whatever good that event may have done to Scotland in other respects, it not only failed to assist in the maintenance or development of the national tongue, but it materially helped to weaken its position by bringing with it the Bible and other religious works in English. The rapid rise of a new and interesting literature in England hastened the process still more, by placing new models before the Scottish authors, scribes, and printers of the day. It

the Scottish Tongue

is surprising how quickly this influence made itself felt. An instance of it can be quite clearly seen in the two manuscripts containing the poems of Sir Richard Maitland (together with those of other Scottish poets). One of these, the folio, was finished in 1582; the other, the quarto, in 1586; and even in these four years the effect of Southern models upon the language and spelling is very clearly marked.

With these preparations, the climax naturally came with the Union of the Crowns. After that date the former equality between the English and Scottish tongues was completely gone, and English was definitely recognised as the standard form for literary work, although the native tongue might persist in colouring it to a greater or less degree according to the taste or learning of the writer.

To a great extent, of course, Scots continued to speak after their own fashion, while trying to write as the English wrote. If this had not been so, the revival of dialect literature towards the end of the seventeenth century would not have been so natural or so easy. It is significant, too, that the precursors of this revival, the Semples of Beltrees, did not belong to the humbler part of the community—showing that the native tongue was still familiar in good society, It was, in fact, still only in a period of quiescence out of which it might have been fully aroused if circumstances had really been favourable, and out of which it did revive to a considerable extent.

In a gathering of Scots it is unnecessary to enter into details regarding the history of Scottish vernacular literature in the eighteenth century, marked as it is with the names of the great triad, Ramsay, Ferguson, and Burns, and with those of many lesser lights. So far as it went, the revival of the native tongue for literary purposes was eminently successful, and the genius of Burns gave it a permanent place among the languages of the world. This was a great achievement, and compensates in no small degree for the loss of prestige which the language had previously sustained.

It is only when we critically examine the range of this Scottish literature of the eighteenth century that the weakness of the position becomes apparent. Of what does it really consist? Mainly of short poems and songs —narrative or lyric verse—of high quality at its best, but (much as we may enjoy it) outside the work of Burns seldom compelling the interest or admiration of those who are not born Scots. There are only a few attempts at longer poetic compositions, such as the "Gentle Shepherd" of Allan Ramsay, or "The Fortunate Shepherdess" of Alexander Ross. Of prose there is very little, and what there is, is of the trivial and humorous type that may serve to amuse, but certainly does nothing to impart dignity to the language in which it is written. It is here that the real nakedness of the situation is most clearly exposed. No Scottish writer of the eighteenth century who had anything important to say in prose attempted to say it in the language of his countrymen. He did it in his best English, and all the time he was haunted by an uneasy feeling that even his choicest English was not free from those dreadful solecisms known as Scotticisms, which would assuredly be pointed out and laughed at when his book had penetrated into the sister-kingdom.

In this respect, then, the eighteenth century

did not mend the faults of the seventeenth ; it made them worse. It helped to establish beyond remedy the feeling that for all serious and practical purposes—for all written and spoken discourses on formal occasions, even for familiar letter writing—the Scottish tongue was no longer admissible. Worse still, it established English as the only form of the language in which instruction was given, while the ability to read or write Scottish was left to be acquired by nature. If you remember what sort of education Burns had, the truth of this will be realized. Schoolmasters, it is true, sometimes continued to use the vernacular even in school, but merely as a matter of habit ; what they were actually engaged in teaching was the reading and the writing of English. All things considered, I have little doubt that the ideas of culture which prevailed in the second half of the eighteenth century are largely responsible for finally reducing our old Lowland tongue to the position of a dialect, from which it has never since recovered.

In saying this, I am not forgetting the Scottish literature of the nineteenth century. During the whole of that period there was

the Scottish Tongue

no lack of good, and even great, Scottish writers who used the native tongue. The strain of poetry never died out, though only now and then attaining the level of the days of Burns, and really represents a remarkably wide-spread knowledge of the Lowland speech and a deep-rooted attachment to it. In prose writing, too, the dialect makes its appearance to an extent undreamed of in the eighteenth century; and its use in novels and tales, from those of Scott down to the most modern short story in the magazine or newspaper, has had immense effect in forcing upon the attention of the world at large the fact that Scotland still has its own way of speaking and of thinking. In these respects, I think there is nothing to complain of or apologise for, unless it be that the editors of the Scottish newspapers have not always been careful to discern between the vernacular and the vulgar, and have frequently allowed a thin veneer of Scottish spelling to pass muster as a genuine representation of the popular speech.

But when we have sufficiently appreciated this aspect of the case, and proceed to consider the situation a little more closely, it must, I think, be granted that all this literature has not altered matters in one material respect—it has not availed either to restore the spoken tongue to a stronger position than it had in the eighteenth century, or even to prevent it from falling still further into disuse. A language cannot live merely by what is written in it, especially if the scope of its written use is limited to poetry or to the dialogue in novels and tales. Even Latin, with all its advantages as a literary medium, ceased at last to be reckoned among the living tongues.

We have, therefore, a problem which occurs elsewhere in Europe at the present day, as I hope to show later on. The language of the country—in this case the Scottish tongue—has steadily receded, and to all appearance is still receding, from actual use in everyday life, from all matters of business or administration, from school and church, and so on, but is still cultivated with success and even with enthusiasm for certain intellectual purposes and on sentimental grounds. How long can these tendencies co-exist without the second becoming purely artificial? That is the problem.

the Scottish Tongue

The question, of course, has two aspects. If Scots practically cease to use their tongue in their everyday talk, a knowledge of its form and vocabulary will soon only be acquired by reading—by a study of the existing literature. This affects both the writers and their readers. When the author has acquired facility in writing a language which he really does not himself employ, can he safely count upon an understanding public of readers whose knowledge of it is similarly artificial ? No doubt this stage will only be arrived at by degrees, but in the end it is bound to come. I think it is not going too far to say that to some extent it has already arrived, and that it would not be difficult in recent Scottish literature to specify books which owe not a little to a close imitation of the older writers, and even a diligent use of the Scottish dictionary.

It is therefore a matter of some importance for those who believe that the Scottish tongue has a national value, to know exactly what the situation now is. It is nearly a quarter of a century since I ceased to live in Scotland, and I feel that I am not sufficiently acquainted with the circumstances of the present day to be perfectly definite on this point. Perhaps some of those present may be able to give useful information from a more recent acquaintance with the actual facts.

From all I can learn, however, the spoken tongue is not holding its own with that " dourness " which we like to think of as particularly Scottish. The schoolmaster, the newspaper and magazine, and the novel, are proving too strong for it—to say nothing of ideas of culture which may be mistaken but are none the less powerful. There is, at least on the surface, sufficient justification for statements that the dialect is declining —even if " dying out " may be too strong an expression. History has shown that it is never quite safe to say that any language or dialect is " dying out." In this respect languages are apt to prove like " threatened men " : they live long. A century after the Norman Conquest we find a historian stating (and probably with truth) that English barely survived as a language of the rustics in out-of-the-way districts. In the middle of the seventeenth century a Frisian scholar contemplated the speedy demise of the Frisian tongue; a Frisian schoolmaster constantly writes to assure me of the same thing at the present day, and this at a time when more Frisian is being written and printed than at any previous date. Even complaints as to the decline of the Scottish tongue are not new. Prefixed to the poems of Andrew Shirrefs, published in 1790, there is a piece written in 1788 entitled "An Address in Scotch, on the Decay of that Language."

This is a matter in which the schoolmaster is not entirely to be trusted, but it would be interesting and valuable to have a collection of reports from Scottish country schoolmasters as to the position which the dialect still holds as a living form of speech —and it would be equally valuable to have a statement of their own attitude towards it. In the past the schoolmaster has usually been indifferent or actually hostile; it would be interesting to know how far that attitude has been modified in Scotland, as it has been in some other countries where similar conditions have prevailed.

From the schoolmaster, too, we might learn how far a knowledge of the native tongue is being maintained among the younger generation by what they read. That this is not being done within the school is certain, so far as I am aware. I have not yet learned that the excellent " Readings in Modern Scots" by Alexander Mackie, published by Messrs. Chambers in 1913, has become a favourite school book, as it richly deserves to be. I am also quite certain that the Scottish " Selections from the Waverley Novels " prepared expressly with a view to being used in schools, and published in 1916, has not yet penetrated within the walls of the school-room. One may, indeed, shrewdly suspect that the intrusion of such reading-books would rather embarrass than delight a considerable number of teachers, male and female, who have been accustomed to consider a careful avoidance, and even a complete ignorance, of their own native tongue as the prime essential towards a state of academic culture.

What then is the position of Scottish literature among the younger generation outside of the schools ? Here, again, the school-master might be able to tell us something. I understand that, in some parts of Scotland at least, school libraries have lately been instituted. It would be interesting to know what proportion of the books in these libraries consist of the standard Scottish authors in poetry or prose. I fancy that we may assume that the more prominent novelists from Scott to the present day are not unrepresented, and that some at least of the poets are included. But I shall be surprised, and delighted, if full consideration has been given to the question of doing justice to the national literature in selecting the books for these libraries, or if definite encouragement has been given towards the reading of the most national authors. On the face of it, this would seem only natural and just, and that there should be any doubt about it is merely a consequence of the whole past history of Scottish education. Our superiority to some other countries in educational matters has been accompanied by one defect—the absolute neglect of the national element in all that relates to language and literature.

I have made these remarks on the assumption that the reports that have reached me in recent years are substantially accurate, and that the younger generation does not have the same hold upon the national tongue, or the same interest in it, as their fathers had. In some respects this estimate is certainly correct. It would be quite safe to assert, for example, that in Forfarshire at the present day there is no piece of Scottish poetry so thoroughly well-known to the population at large as Beattie's " John o' Arnha " was about the middle of last century. Scottish poetry and the Scottish portions of novels and tales, may still be read with understanding and enjoyment, but they are not the main literary interest now as the corresponding poems and stories were to many of the earlier generation.

There are, however, some allowances to be made here. It must be remembered that the rising generation is still absolutely fresh from an intensive system of education in which their home language has had no place —from which in fact, it has been carefully excluded—while their education in that dialect is still incomplete. Those old folks whose rich store of real Scottish words and phrases even yet is so delightful, did not acquire them all before they had reached the age of fourteen. My own experience

the Scottish Tongue

is that one goes on learning new Scottish words and phrases as long as one lives; and I have no doubt that this fact will continually operate to prevent the dialect from giving way as rapidly as the apparent symptoms would lead one to expect. I am also convinced that with advancing years there is a steady, though unconscious, tendency to adopt older habits of speech, so that the grandson in course of time comes to talk much more like his grandfather than he did in his earlier years. This, in fact, is one of the reasons why languages do not change more rapidly from one generation to another.

We must also be careful not to generalize too hastily in another way. Even among the older generation of dialect-speakers, whose opportunities of learning it in a pure form were much greater, there are very great differences both in the knowledge of the dialect and in the ability to use it correctly. Anyone who is really familiar with the rural population of Scotland will recognize the truth of this. The language of some speakers is an inexhaustible store of expressive words and phrases. They seem never to speak for any length of time without bringing in a fine old word or turn of speech which one has never heard them use before, but which comes out as naturally and as aptly as if it were an every-day expression. On the other hand, their next-door neighbour may have a limited, common-place, colourless vocabulary, entirely devoid of any picturesque or unexpected element. This being so with the older speakers, we cannot expect every boy or girl, or even every young man or young woman, to exhibit a full knowledge and perfect command even of their own local dialect, to say nothing of the Scottish tongue as a whole. What knowledge of English would most English country children have, if they learned no more of it at school than they do at home? Accordingly, when we try to forecast the future of the Scottish tongue by comparing the young with the old, we must be sure that the basis of comparison is quite a fair one.

Supposing, however, that those who assert the decline and ultimate disappearance of Scottish as a living form of speech are right in their view, what effect will it have

the Scottish Tongue

upon the people of Scotland? I have no doubt that for some persons of a practical unsentimental turn of mind the prospect will excite no grave anxiety, and that they may even contend, with some show of reason, that the result will in some respects be a positive gain. Modern conditions of life, they may argue, are adverse to the continuance of anything that savours of provincialism, and the young Scot who is not impeded by having to divest himself of his local speech will have a better start in the world at large. There may be an element of truth in this—though it is surprising how Scots have succeeded in the past in evading the terrible consequences arising from a Scottish accent. It is, however, a question whether the same result might not be more legitimately attained by drawing a clearer distinction between Scottish and English modes of speech, and improving the teaching of the latter. It will be no gain at all to the Scottish youth to have lost the vocabulary of his national tongue, if he still acquires from his parents, his schoolmates, and even from his teacher, the local intonation which will identify him wherever he goes. If the better teaching of English in the schools of Scotland is something desirable—and I have nothing to say against it—it is by no means certain that the end will most surely be attained by first effacing the national tongue. It will certainly not be the speediest means: the history of all languages in recent times goes to prove that. If, however, the end is attained by such means, it must be frankly recognized that to that extent it implies a denationalization of the Scottish people. A nation which has no distinctive language lacks one of the most obvious features of nationality, and one which has lost its own language has to that extent allowed itself to become an appendage to another.

This truth is very clearly expressed in a Frisian song, written some sixty years ago, when the Frisians began to take active steps to protect their language: "We will not let our language go," it says, "for without the Frisian tongue there are Frisians no more."

If, however, the force of circumstances should justify the arguments of the practical unsentimental person, and a first-hand knowledge of Scottish should practically dis-

the Scottish Tongue

appear in the course of the next generation or two, what effect will this have in relation to Scottish literature? Clearly it will create a new situation in this respect. Either the production of new literature in the dialect will cease altogether, or it will become a mere artificial form of composition, which will no longer have even the merit of local colouring, unless the scene is laid in the past. Even at the present day I could name an excellent scholar and critic born and bred in Scotland, who is inclined to believe that no man writes Scottish naturally, that its employment for poetry or prose is merely a conscious effort towards attaining a certain literary effect and not at all due to any natural impulse to use the tongue which lies nearest to him. I do not accept this view as absolutely correct even now, but we must certainly rapidly come to that stage if the written tongue has no longer the spoken one behind it.

We shall have this anomalous situation. Scotland will continue to exist, and the glory of its past literature no man can take from it. But the Scottish people, having ceased to speak its own language, will be no more capable of understanding and enjoying that literature than any other portion of the English-speaking world. The Scot who wishes to read Burns will have to use the glossary as diligently as the Englishman of the present day; and I cannot readily imagine a more humiliating situation for a nation than to depend on a glossary for the understanding of its national poet. Worse still, the Scot will no longer, except by special training, be able to read aloud his national literature without mangling it in the most heart-rending (or ear-rending) manner. We have all, in our time, known what it is to hear Scottish poetry read, or a Scottish joke told, by one not born in Scotland, and we know how impossible it is for him to come anywhere near the real thing. But that is exactly what the Scot of the future will do if Scottish ceases to be a current form of speech—unless indeed the literature is buried along with the language.

Perhaps even that would come in time, for does anyone suppose that the literature could really be understood and appreciated to the full if the meaning of the words had to be learned from a glossary? Any Scot

the Scottish Tongue

of the present day may be confronted with words which are unknown to him either because they have gone out of use, or because they are not employed in his own dialect. But so long as he is familiar with the staple of the language as a whole, no strange word can wholly disconcert him or prevent him from appreciating the point of what he reads or hears. It will be a very different thing when all words and forms not found in standard English are equally unfamiliar, and imply an effort to understand. Even the simplest phrases, of course, have frequently acquired subtle associations which cannot be explained by anyone who has not known them in their proper setting from his earliest years. It would be quite easy to illustrate this from a few of the masterpieces of Scottish literature; but it will make the point equally clear, if one or two examples are taken from the lighter field of Scottish anecdote—an experiment which every Scot ought to be able to make for himself.

Such examples, trivial as they may be, illustrate what will happen to a great deal of Scottish literature, if the living tongue is no longer there to vivify the words and phrases, and bring their full meaning home to the mind of the reader, without a moment's pause, and with the exact shade of meaning which the author intended them to have.

I need not insist on the wealth of idiom and melody that will thus be lost; that will easily be understood by anyone to whom Scottish literature is at all familiar. That countless expressive phrases will cease to be expressive is obvious, because no exact equivalent for them can be found in standard English. At the same time this argument must not be pressed too far. Scottish is not necessarily superior to English because it has untranslatable words and phrases. The same merit can be claimed for any language and any dialect, however inferior it may be in its general character. If pushed to extremes, the claim to possess words which have no exact equivalent in English might provoke the retort given to a Danish lady, who was expatiating at too great length on the expressiveness of a Danish word meaning " tiresome " or " tedious " (in the most exalted degree). " Well, after all, Denmark is the only country where you want that word."

the Scottish Tongue

That the native speech of Scotland, however, when at its best, is a rich, euphonious and expressive tongue is a powerful reason for not readily letting it go, and adds weight to the equally strong argument of an historic right to possess this language and a moral duty to preserve it. What, after all, is the Scottish tongue, historically considered? It is the language which, though first brought in by an invading race, the Angles, had by the fourteenth century been adopted over the greater part of the area which it now covers. From that date, and in some parts from a much earlier date, it has been handed down from father to son, from mother to daughter, in an unbroken line. Generation after generation it has served to express all that men and women, young men and maidens, lads and lasses, have had to say to each other from their childhood to their later years. In it they have talked of the tasks and trials of everyday life, of their joys and sorrows, of their hopes and fears, of everything that concerned themselves and their surroundings. In that way the language has come to partake of their character; it has been a part and parcel of the Scottish people, from which it cannot be dissevered without loss. It has been the work of centuries to frame this speech, the labour has been justified by the results, and no other tongue can fully take its place. Are the reasons (whatever they may be) for letting it go of any weight against these considerations?

So far as I can make out, the spoken tongue in Scotland has changed very little since the end of the sixteenth century. This is considerably disguised by the old conventional spelling which persists long after 1600, but when one penetrates behind this the substantial identity with the speech of the present day becomes apparent. With the new spelling which accompanied the literary revival in the end of the seventeenth century, the identity with that of the present day becomes unmistakable. For more than three centuries, then, the Scottish people, under all the adverse influences of church, school, and general culture, has preserved in substantially the same form this heritage from the past, without realizing that there was any merit in doing so. Now that the value of thus preserving the national tongue is coming to be realized (as it is already recognized in some other countries), it is incumbent on every thinking and patriotic Scot to consider what can be done to assist in so urgent and delicate a task. There is here both a Scylla and a Charybdis : indifference on the one hand and artificiality on the other.

In what I have to say next I labour under the disadvantage of not having heard Mr. Will's address on " the Preservation of the Scottish Vernacular," to which I have no doubt many of you listened on November 22. On that account I am afraid that I may to a considerable extent be traversing the same ground. If, however, our views agree, there is all the more likelihood of our being right ; and if we differ, I have no doubt that the right course can yet be discovered.

My first suggestion is, that it is not necessary to treat this problem as if it were peculiar to Scotland, and consequently to work out a complete plan of campaign from the beginning. The same problem, how to revive a declining national tongue, has presented itself in recent years in several countries in Europe, and has there received either a partial or a complete solution. It is, therefore, only natural and practical to inquire into the methods pursued in these countries, and try to ascertain how far they are applicable to our own case. For this purpose I shall quote part of an address which I gave to the Yorkshire Dialect Society in 1912.

"During the course of the nineteenth century a considerable number of European countries have witnessed remarkable instances of new life in forms of speech which seemed to be slowly giving way under the pressure of more highly-developed, or at least more highly-organized, languages. The position of the small languages, and of many dialects within the larger ones, is very different now from what it was a hundred years ago; in many cases it amounts to a new lease of life, and of some it might almost be said that they have only begun to live now. I need only mention the cases of Catalan in Spain, of Provençal and Breton in France, of Bohemian and Hungarian in Austria, of Flemish in Belgium, to show how widespread the tendency has been. Several causes have nearly always contributed to the revival, but the mainsprings in every case have been a renewal of national or local feeling on the one hand, and the study of philology and folklore on the other. In some cases, at least, the latter cause has preceded and even created the former; the knowledge of having a language of its own has been the first step towards the consciousness of being a nation. Wherever this has been the process, the revival has, in the first place, been a literary one, and in some cases it has gone no further; in others, the literary impulse has acted powerfully upon the practical use of the language, and has recovered much of the ground previously lost.

" To make this clearer than can be done by general statements, I shall briefly explain what has happened in the case of one or two languages lying very near to our own. The facts are interesting in themselves, and I think there are some lessons to be drawn from them.

" When the three Germanic tribes from the other side of the North Sea invaded Britain in the fifth century, they left behind them a closely-related people, speaking almost the very same language, viz.: the Frisians.

The Present State of

It seems possible that some of these actually did accompany their kinsmen to their country, but the Frisian people as a whole remained where it was. As time went on, they suffered encroachment from the Frankish and Saxon tribes lying to the south and east of them, and the area over which Frisian was spoken was gradually lessened and finally broken up. At the present time it is represented by most of the province of Friesland in the Netherlands, by a small district in the province of Oldenburg in Germany, and by the west coast of Slesvig and the adjacent islands. The total number of those who now speak Frisian is somewhere about 250,000. The old Frisians had practically no literature; 'they were afraid of nothing so much as pen and ink,' one of their modern authors has said. With the exception of one poet in the seventeenth century they succeeded in living down to the nineteenth without producing anything remarkable in this direction. From the sixteenth century onwards Dutch was the official language in West Friesland, and was regularly employed in church and school. In the seventeenth century we find a Frisian scholar expressing

the Scottish Tongue

his fears that the mother-tongue might soon be extinct. He underestimated, however, the conservatism of the Frisian character, which does not so readily change old ways for new. When the second quarter of the nineteenth century began, Frisian was not only still a living tongue, daily spoken by nearly all the country-people in Friesland, but it actually began to develop a literature. This has steadily increased in volume, and in some respects has improved in quality, and I am sure that most persons not already acquainted with the facts would be greatly surprised to discover how many Frisian books have been printed during the last half-century. A society founded in 1846, and still active, did much to further the literary movement. Within recent years new and important steps have been taken which deserve mention. It had become doubtful to some interested observers whether even Frisian conservatism would be able, under modern conditions, to preserve the language from declining; whether it could much longer offer an effective resistance to improved education and increased means of communication. Measures have accordingly been taken to improve its chances by providing instruction in it in the public schools, but entirely as a voluntary subject for both teachers and scholars. Excellent school-books have been prepared for this purpose, and a special fund has been organized to provide both the books and the teaching. It is too soon as yet to foretell what the result may be, but the action is clearly on the right lines. Still another point. Frisian, like Scottish, has suffered from the fact that at the Reformation no translation of the Bible was made in it. Every effort is now being made to supply this want, and within the past year or two a religious society on a Frisian basis has been formed. It ought also to be mentioned that amateur acting of Frisian plays has become very general and immensely popular, not only in Friesland itself, but also in the Frisian societies which have been formed in all the leading towns of the Netherlands. Whatever another century may bring, it is quite clear that during the present generation at least West Frisian will go forward and flourish on these lines.

"The practical result of a literary revival

of this kind can be better estimated by observing what has happened in recent years in Norway. In that country the native language, which had been largely used for literary purposes in the thirteenth century, began, for political reasons, to give way to Danish, and from about 1500 Norwegian practically ceased to be written at all. During the seventeenth and eighteenth centuries only scanty specimens of it are to be found, and these are rather of linguistic than of literary interest. Among the educated classes, and in the towns, even the spoken language was largely modified under Danish influence, though it still retained many Norwegian peculiarities of sound and expression. About 1840, however, a young Norwegian, Ivar Aasen, began to study the real Norwegian dialects which were still spoken in the country districts, and to collect their special vocabulary. He was agreeably surprised to find that these dialects had preserved to a remarkable extent the forms and words of the classical old Norwegian, and before long the idea came to him that it was still possible to build up out of them a national language, and thus restore to Norway the full use of its native tongue.

With Aasen himself, and his immediate followers, the progress in this direction was slow, and the idea met with the strongest opposition from many quarters. The movement, however, steadily grew, and about twenty-five years ago it began to be a serious question whether Norway as a whole was to adopt this new Norwegian tongue or not. The question is far from settled yet, but the advocates of "Landsmaal" have already made surprising progress and have scored some signal victories. They have succeeded in making Landsmaal a school-subject, and even a University one: they have produced a very large body of literature, some of it of high quality, and much of it of great national interest. It is no longer possible to learn all that is worth knowing about Norway, unless one can read works written in this form of Norwegian, and for the study of the local dialects it is absolutely indispensable. It has already had a great influence upon the Danish written in Norway, and whatever the end may be, it is quite certain that in another generation the literary language of Norway, even in its least local form, will be something quite distinct from

Danish. This is a remarkable result of philological interest combined with strong national feeling, and it well illustrates the impossibility of predicting what such a movement may lead to. A century ago even the most acute observer would have said that as a literary language Norwegian had been dead for centuries, and had no prospects whatever of a resurrection. His opinion would have been quite justifiable, for even at the present day there are many Norwegians who will not allow themselves to be convinced by what has already been accomplished.

" I need not go multiplying examples from various countries, but there is one instance which I should still like to mention —that of the language spoken in the Faroes. This is in its origin a Norwegian dialect, and in olden times (after it became distinct from Norwegian) was never written at all. It developed, however, a very extensive and very remarkable ballad literature, and about the close of the eighteenth century a beginning was made in writing this down. During the nineteenth century attempts to write Faroese prose began to be made, and within the past fifty years or so it has gradually been raised to the position of a literary language. If we remember that for several centuries the official language in the Faroes was Danish, and that this language was exclusively employed in church and school, and if we further consider the smallness of the population (only 15,000 now and formerly much less) this change in the position of the native tongue is something remarkable. With Faroese, as with Norwegian, the situation is absolutely different from what it was a century ago. At that time it would have been hard to convince anyone that the language could be used for any other form of literature than the native ballad; now one may find it in interesting accounts of Faroese life and customs, plays dealing with local history, school-books, a good grammar of the language for school use, a work on botany, and even an excellent novel. All this is but another illustration of what may result from work that at the outset has a scholarly, rather than a practical, character."

From these examples, which in several respects offer close parallels to the case of Scotland, we can learn several powerful factors

the Scottish Tongue

in the revival of a language: first, school-teaching and school-books; second, cheap and popular books in the language of the people; third, scholarly work in the history of the language, and in the preparation of vocabularies and dictionaries; fourth, the cultivation of a new and national literature.

Let us now see how far these factors are at work for the preservation (to say nothing of a revival) of the Scottish tongue:—

1. The teaching of Scottish in schools. There are several books and many reports on Scottish education; but I am afraid that in any of these a section with this heading will be uncommonly like the famous chapter " On snakes in Iceland."

To cope with this, I would suggest that the Vernacular Circle of the London Burns Club should prepare a memorial on the subject, and send it to the Scottish Education Department. If backed up by signatories of sufficient note, such a memorial might have some effect. If not, it would at least clear the way for the adoption of the Frisian method, viz., the voluntary co-operation of teachers and pupils in the study of the native tongue, for which I have no

The Present State of

doubt that the active support of many Burns clubs and Caledonian societies could be obtained.

As to school-books. I have already mentioned that at least two exist, and to provide others would be a simple task. I, myself, am in a position to hand another to the printers as soon as any publisher can be persuaded to undertake it. But until the Education Department is converted, or circumvented, I quite understand the publisher's point of view. A school-book which is not used in any school is not a business proposition.

2. What opportunity has the mass of the Scottish people at the present day of reading literature in its own tongue? Of the older writers—practically only Burns and Scott. Of the more modern writers—cheap editions of some popular novels. Otherwise only the poetry and prose of the Scottish column in a weekly newspaper, of varying merit, but frequently of a nature to lower the prestige of the vernacular instead of raising it. No doubt other works are available for those who are really bent on obtaining them; but of many of the older writers

no modern popular edition exists at all, and many have been so scarce that a copy is rarely to be found even in the hands of collectors. For the early period of Scottish literature the absence of cheap modern editions is conspicuous, and so far as the people at large is concerned all the old Scottish " makers " from Barbour to Montgomery might just as well never have written a line. Even in the eighteenth century it was otherwise, and at that time it was still possible to print popular editions of the Wallace and of Sir David Lyndsay.

Here, again, a large field of enterprise awaits the various societies which have the welfare of the Scottish tongue at heart. To assist in the publication and the dissemination of really popular editions of the older Scottish writers would be rendering an immense service to the cause of the Scottish tongue—for no language can really be independent of its past, and least of all one which has allowed itself to become impoverished in recent times.

3. The study of the modern Scottish tongue, I am glad to say, is not being neglected. Since the Scots Dialect Com-

mittee was formed some twelve years ago, much information has been collected both as to the vocabulary and the phonetics of the various dialects, and the material thus brought together is being gradually published by Mr. William Grant. This is a work in which every Scot can take a part, and even the smallest contributions may have their value.

Quite recently, Sir James Wilson made a valuable study of the dialect of Lower Strathearn. I mention this not merely for its own merits, but to emphasize the fact that the publication of this special study of a Scottish dialect was encouraged, not by any Scottish association, but by the Philological Society which has its headquarters in London, and numbers very few Scots among its members.

I am certain that much more might be done by the Scottish societies which exist all over the world to encourage work of the kind. As things are at present, the actual work has to be done for pure love of the subject, and publication is a matter of difficulty and uncertainty. For the printing of the material it has collected,

the Scottish Tongue

the Scots Dialect Committee has to depend on grants from the Carnegie Trust, and it is largely the guarantee of support from that source which will make possible the publication of a new and thorough account of the dialect of Roxburghshire. This work, by Mr. George Watson, has not been done on the Borders, but in Oxford, though with the co-operation of many correspondents now living in, or natives of, the county. Knowing the enthusiasm with which Mr. Watson has carried out this undertaking, and the amount of honest and discriminating work he has put into it, I feel that if interest in the Scottish tongue were as prevalent and as genuine as it ought to be, the successful publication of such a work could not be in doubt for a moment.

Incidentally, I may remind you that Oxford has already done no small service to the cause of the Scottish tongue. It was there that Professor Wright produced his indispensable " English Dialect Dictionary " with its wealth of Scottish material; it was there that the Rev. Mr. Warrack compiled his useful " Scots Dialect Dictionary," although it was published in Edinburgh; it was at the Clarendon Press that Sir James Wilson's study of the Strathearn dialect was printed; and it was the Clarendon Press which published the Scottish Selections from the Waverley Novels that I have already mentioned. For the older period of the language, also, the "Oxford English Dictionary" forms an indispensable addition to Jamieson—a fact which does not yet appear to be sufficiently realized north of the Tweed. I frequently receive letters from Scotland asking for an explanation of some old word which the inquirer has not found in Jamieson. In most cases the word has already been fully dealt with in the Oxford Dictionary, sometimes twenty or thirty years ago, but it has evidently never occurred to the inquirer that he might find it there.

Even with the Oxford Dictionary, however, there is still room for a special dictionary of the older period of the Scottish tongue, from the fourteenth to the latter part of the seventeenth century. For some years I have been making preparations for this work; and when the time arrives for setting about it in earnest, I trust to my countrymen at home and abroad to insure that the under-

the Scottish Tongue

taking will not strand for want of active support.

4. There is still room for a much wider use of the Scottish tongue in literature. In poetry, there is a lack of longer poems of a serious character such as Ross attempted in his " Fortunate Shepherdess," but naturally of a type more suited to the taste of the present day. There is a lack of drama, whether in verse, like the " Gentle Shepherd," or in ordinary prose. When one considers the plays that have been recently written in dialects of the North of England, when one looks at the amazing list of popular plays written and acted in Friesland during the past half-century, one feels how far Scotland has failed to develop this form of literature, which almost more than any other admits of being really popular in character, and (as has clearly been shown in Friesland) can be of the greatest value in awakening a real enthusiasm for the use of the national tongue. A well-constructed dialect play has a wider and more direct appeal than any other form of literature, except a song. It is easy to understand; it deals with familiar scenes and uses the very speech of the spec-

tators; but in the hands of a true artist it can be used to dignify that everyday tongue and bring out its best qualities. There is assuredly a great work lying before the younger Scottish writers, if they will only cultivate this form of literature.

Scottish narrative prose, too, requires to be developed on other lines than those practised hitherto. In the counties which I have already mentioned, and in others that might be included, it was formerly the custom to use the native speech only for the dialogue of novels and tales, in the way with which we are so familiar in the Scottish novelists. But all of them have now gone beyond that stage, and not only the dialogue, but the narrative part of the tales as well, is now commonly written in the national tongue. We still want to see that done in Scotland. It is with feelings of admiration, mixed with envy, that I see this continually being done in such languages as Frisian, Low German, the new Norwegian, and even in the late-born Faroese, while Scotland still lags behind, though its revival antedates theirs by at least a century and a half.

I might say something of more serious

forms of literature, which even the smallest of these tongues can now exhibit, but I shall content myself with merely indicating this aspect of the subject. Can you imagine a complete grammar of Lowland Scots, written throughout in that language? The Frisians and the Faroese have done that for their tongues. Can you imagine a work on Botany written throughout in the Scottish tongue? There is one in Faroese. If anyone doubts the possibility of recreating a literary tongue, capable of expressing all the necessary ideas which must occur in dealing with literature, history, science, and even philosophy, I will direct him to what has been written in the new Norwegian tongue within the past twenty years. He will there find the triumphant refutation of all that the sceptics allege against the mere possibility of such a language.

We have had the beginnings of this already in Scotland, but they have failed to bear fruit, perhaps because the wrong subjects and methods were chosen. Hately Waddell's versions of the Psalms and Isaiah were remarkable achievements, and in many ways illustrate the capacity of the Scottish

The Present State of the Scottish Tongue

tongue for exalted subjects, but they were too hard for the majority of the people. The experience of other countries has clearly shown that in the revival of a language it is absolutely needful to "creep afore ye gang" and that "huly and fairly" is likely to come better speed than too ambitious efforts at the outset.

Some Scottish Characteristics

By JOHN BUCHAN, M.A., LL.D.

Delivered at the Scots Corporation Hall, Crane Court, Fleet Street, London, on February 7, 1921.

IT is sometimes a good thing to stop considering other people for a little and to consider ourselves. You and I are Scotsmen, members of a famous race, and it might be worth our while to consider what that race is and what it means. Now this is a case where I think we had better not follow Burns's petition :—

"O wad some power the giftie gie us
To see oursels as ithers see us!"

For I am convinced that others see us all wrong. A caricature of a Scotsman has firmly fixed itself in English minds. Over the Border, they imagine, we are always pawky, and canny, always "hoastin" and "pechin," that we are not very often sober, and that most of our time is spent in discussing theology and trying to "do" our neighbours. A great many people, too, imagine that we all wear kilts on weekdays and funeral blacks on the Sabbath, that our meals consist entirely of porridge and haggis, and that our only recreations from the stern business of life are whisky, Burns's poems, sermons, and the bagpipes. That is the Cockney notion of Scotsmen. You will find it in bad novels and stupid music-halls. But,

Some Scottish Characteristics

of course, you and I know that it is ridiculously unlike the truth. No, we will let the Giftie alone. We will try to see ourselves, not as others see us, for they know nothing about it, but as we really are. We are a separate people, very different from our neighbours, and I do not believe that anything is going to make us alike. But these differences lie much deeper than many imagine. We are entering upon a new Scotland, which in superficial things is less distinct than the old. We are losing, for example, our old language. How many people nowadays can speak that beautiful soft tongue, the true Lowland Scots? A few herds in Megget or Ettrick, but even with these the old words are dying out. You will always be able to tell a Scotsman by his speech, but it will be by his accent and not by his language, just as you can tell a man from Lancashire or Essex. Then we have little Scottish vernacular literature left. Who is there to-day who can write Scotch verse as Fergusson and Hogg, and even as Stevenson wrote it? Few indeed!

We have lost, too, our system of education. Elementary schools on the same model as England have taken the place of the old

Some Scottish Characteristics

parish school. Fifty years ago a boy in the better-off classes went to a grammar school, and then to a Scots university. Now he goes to an English public school, and then to Oxford or Cambridge. We have all got the same kind of cheap books and newspapers, and if a touch of nature makes the whole world kin, so does a halfpenny paper. Scottish theology, again, the old, grim doctrinal theology of our grandfathers, is not what it was. Few people are interested in it; few people care to dispute on some tough matter of dogma. A Scots sermon is getting very much like an English sermon, only, if I may say so, considerably better. We have "instrumental" music and "human" hymn books in our churches, and we neither sit at the singing nor stand at the prayers. We are becoming a temperate nation, too, which is a very good thing. Really, we are getting horribly like our neighbours. The old days have gone, and we can never wile them back. Very soon, I am afraid, an Englishman will not be able to connect a Scotsman with the Scots language, or Scots theology, or even Scots drink. But we shall still be different—very different; not in

Some Scottish Characteristics

externals, perhaps, but in the things that matter, our characters and our minds. Now, what is the secret of this difference? What are the true Scottish characteristics? That is what I want you to look at to-night.

We are all agreed that Scotsmen are a separate people. But what made us a people? I think you will find that hard to answer, for you will find few of the forces present which give a people unity. It is not common race. We have between the Mull of Galloway and John o' Groat's at least three great race-stocks—Saxon, Norse, and Celtic. I myself and some of you are Lowlanders, of precisely the same blood as the people of Northumberland and Yorkshire, and we are cut off by the widest gulf from the people of the Highlands. When I am at home, the Highlands, much as I love them, always seem a little like a foreign country, and their people a foreign people. But when I meet a man from Sutherland and a man from Northumberland in some foreign land I feel, I do not know why, that the Gaelic-speaking Highlander is one of my own folk, and the Northumbrian, who speaks

Some Scottish Characteristics

almost with my own accent, is not. Nor is the secret of unity a common Church. We have all kinds of Churches in Scotland, and even within the Presbyterian communion we have violent differences. It is not so very long ago that you could find a Highland minister classing U. P.'s with Mormons and Mohammedans as among those who would have a bad time at the Judgment Day. Even nowadays, when we all talk of union, there are some pretty big barriers to be crossed. Nor, lastly, is it that which is perhaps the greatest uniter of mankind, a common economic interest. Where will you find a bigger difference of economic interest than between the crofters of the Lews, the miners of Lanarkshire, and the mill-workers of Galashiels ? If occupation determines character, there is little chance of a common strain here. If we want the cause why all Scots, over and above their differences, have certain common characteristics, a common Scottishness, I think we must seek it in our history.

What is the history of Scotland ? In the first place it is the history of a very poor nation. We have not been blessed by Provi-

Some Scottish Characteristics

dence with a rich soil or an agreeable climate. Until a hundred years or so ago, when we discovered the wealth that lies below the soil, we had no means of getting rich. We need not go very far back—only to the eighteenth century, about the time when Prince Charlie and his Highlanders were marching South to try for the throne. I have a great-uncle still living who, when he was a little boy in Tweeddale, remembers talking to an old woman who as a girl had seen Prince Charlie pass; so there is somebody still alive who has talked to somebody who remembered the days I am speaking of. Well, we possess several descriptions of eighteenth-century Scotland from the point of view of English travellers, and what struck them all was the amazing poverty of the people. The roads were few and bad, the crops were poor to one accustomed to English farming, and the travellers spent all their time wondering how such a barren land could support a population at all. The labourers, they tell us, never saw meat, except now and then in the shape of braxy mutton. They lived on different forms of brose and bear-meal porridge and sowens.

Some Scottish Characteristics

(I wonder how many here have eaten sowens? I have, and it is not a bad dish, but I should not call it very sustaining. The best description of it I know is that given by a man who was lost in the moors of Galloway and was entertained at a herd's cottage. He said that the wife " put on some dirty water to boil, and by the blessing of the Lord it turned into a pudden.")

But what really surprised those travellers was the poverty of the gentry. Accustomed to English manor houses with flower gardens and lawns, and fine old furniture and pictures, they expected to find the same kind of thing in the houses of the great families they had heard so much of—the Dundases, the Drummonds, and the Murrays. Instead, they found grim little stone houses with small rooms and narrow windows, and trees planted thick around for shelter against the winter winds. They found the farmyard close to the house, the kitchen-midden under the dining-room windows, and a pig or two routing around the front door. They complained that the food was abominable, and that the only good thing was the claret. I am afraid that our ancestors were not a

Some Scottish Characteristics

very tidy race; like Stevenson's Weir of Hermiston they had "no call to be bonny," for it took them all their time to keep a roof over their heads. In the towns it was worse. We all know what the High Street of Edinburgh was like two hundred years ago, when a Duke of Queensberry, or some other great officer of State, as he walked along it had to keep a good look out in case he got his fine clothes spoiled by one of his own servants emptying the slops from a window of the tenement where he lived. All classes were the same. The great Earl of Mansfield, who was the son of a Scotch peer, and became Lord Chief Justice of England, used to go bare-foot from his home to the school in Perth to save shoe-leather. Poverty is the first and biggest fact in our history, and from that poverty the Scottish race learned certain qualities which only come from a hard school. It learned that nothing comes without effort, and that we value most what costs us most. The homes our forefathers made for themselves were hard won, and therefore they were deeply loved, for love of home has always been a notable Scottish quality. The fireside is all the

Some Scottish Characteristics

cheerier for the black weather out of doors and the long hard day in the rain. Then again, poverty teaches self-reliance and effort. It hardens the fibre of a man and toughens his character. And most of all, it makes a man take risks in life. The more comfortable we are the more likely we are to be sluggish and unenterprising and timid. The complaint against Moab in the Bible is that she was "settled upon her lees." The Bible thought very little of the comfortable man.

The second great fact in Scottish history is its unsettlement. The last wars in Great Britain were fought on her soil. England, you may say, has been at peace ever since the Restoration. But in Scotland we had the long strife of the Covenant, we had Dundee's campaign, which ended at Killiecrankie, we had the Jacobite wars of 1715 and 1745. And for generations before that you had Scotland a kind of cockpit. In most of the English shires there has been no fighting since the Wars of the Roses. Hence a peaceful society grew up and unfortified manor houses were built as early as the sixteenth century. But Scotland had no rest. More than once

Some Scottish Characteristics

an English army marched to the walls of Edinburgh. A herd in Teviotdale never went to bed without the possibility of being roused to defend his master's cattle, amid blazing ricks and roof-trees, against a foray from Northumberland. That was for the Southern Lowlands, while in the Northern Lowlands there was the same risk of attack from the Highland glens. Till a late period in her history Scotland was perpetually being emptied from vessel to vessel. I think such a discipline could only have one result. Dwellers on a border are proverbially a bold race, and the whole of Scotland in this sense was a border. If poverty made us hard and careful, the ancient unsettlement of our land made us enterprising and adventurous.

It is to our history that we must look for the source of what seem to me the two master elements in the Scottish character, as we have seen it in history and as we know it to-day. These elements are hard-headedness on the one hand and romance on the other: common sense and sentiment: practicality and poetry: business and idealism. The two are often thought to be incompatible, but

Some Scottish Characteristics

this is wrong. Almost everybody has got a little of both. It is the peculiarity of the Scottish race that it has both in a high degree. A Baillie Nicol Jarvie will grip the red-hot coulter of a plough and singe the plaid of a Highland cataran; and the Gifted Gilfillan, in " Waverley," after discoursing on the New Jerusalem of the Saints, turns readily and with equal gusto to the price of beasts at Mauchline Fair.

We will take the prosaic side first. We Scotsmen are a commonplace folk, fond of sticking close to the ground, and asking a reason for things and a practical justification. We take a pleasure, a malicious pleasure, I am afraid, in pricking bubbles; and, though we are very sentimental ourselves, we like to pour cold water on other people's sentiment. You remember the shepherd to whom a tourist was dilating on the beauties of a certain hill. " Why, from the top of it," said the tourist, " you can see Ireland." " Ye can see far further than that," said the shepherd, " you can see the mune." We are not very good people to show off before, for some of us seem to have taken an

Some Scottish Characteristics

oath to admire nothing which is not our own.

If an American shows us Niagara, we mention something about Cowie's Linn, and if somebody talks about the Ganges at Calcutta, we observe that it cannot be so fine as the Tweed at Peebles. Now, there is a good side and a bad side to this characteristic. A perpetual tendency to belittle everything that is not your own makes a very unpleasant fellow, the kind of man whom we call in Scotland " nesty." Some of you may have read that wonderful novel of Scottish life called " The House with the Green Shutters." In that book you will find the " nesty " Scot portrayed in all his varieties. When news comes that Jock So-and-so from the village has won the Victoria Cross, all the " nesty " body says is, " Jock So-and-so! There's naething in him. I ken a' about him. His granny keepit a sweetie-shop."

But there is a good side, too, to it, an honesty, a homeliness, a good sense, which in these days, when sentiment runs riot and everybody wears his heart on his sleeve, is a quality beyond price. It is a kind of self-respect, the self-respect of the man who values his own sacred things too highly to gush about them in public. I always think that the finest instance of this admirable reticence is the remark of the mother of Sir David Baird, the great Indian soldier, when she heard that her son's regiment had been captured by Hyder Ali and were chained man to man in his dungeons. All that wonderful old lady said was, " God pity the man that is chained to oor Davie." A Scotsman may admire a thing deeply, but his first thought is for its practical use, like the Lowland farmer who went into St. Paul's Cathedral and stared for some minutes at the immense dome. He then observed to his friend, " Man, it wad haud a terrible lot of hay."

Even in the presence of death this quality does not desert us, for you remember Dean Ramsay's story of the old woman who was dying while a storm was raging round the house. Her last words were : " Sic a night to be fleein' through the air." And you find the best instance of all in the beautiful old ballad of " Annan Water," where the poet tells how the lover was drowned in its flood. The last verse is this :

Some Scottish Characteristics

> And wae betide ye, Annan Water,
> I vow ye are a drumlie river!
> But over thee I'll build a bridge,
> That ye nae mair true love may sever.

The last thought is not of the tragedy of love and death, but of the necessity of preventing it happening again; he will build a brig.

On the commonplace side of our nature, then, we are all inclined to be prosaic and practical. In the next place we are a logical people. I don't mean merely logical in the narrow sense of the word, though we are that also. Where else will you find country people in their conversation using logical divisions, such as "pairtly" this, and "pairtly" that. You remember the story of a Southern tourist who met a bare-footed girl and asked her, "My good woman, do all the women in these parts go bare-foot?" The answer was, "Pairtly, and pairtly we mind our ain business." We are logical, because we always look for a cause for every effect, and are quick to detect fallacies.

I am not sure that this logical grip is not slackening. When people paid more attention to the Shorter Catechism and less to the evening paper it had a better chance of flourishing. But besides being logical in the narrow sense, the Scot is logical in the bold and uncompromising character of his attitude towards the things of the mind. He will not be put off with authorities, however august. I remember an old shoe-maker in Fife who was a great theologian. He was always discussing points of theology, and on one occasion his opponent quoted St. Paul against him. " True," said the old man, " but that's just where me and Paul differs."

You see this in the way in which we regard our Governments. I always like the customary Scotch prayer for those set in authority over us. " Bless, O Lord, the High Court of Parliament now assembled, and overrule their deliberations for the people's good." " Overrule," mark you, not " guide " or " assist "; the assumption being that such deliberations are quite certain to be wrong. You see it in the boldness with which the old Scotch divines used to treat sacred things. There is a sermon by a famous Covenanting minister in which the work of salvation is likened to a game of golf between God and the devil,

Some Scottish Characteristics

with the human soul for the ball. If I were to quote it to you, you would think it shockingly blasphemous, but the man who preached that sermon was one of the saints of his time, and his hearers saw no blasphemy in it. You see this boldness, too, in the way in which the older school of ministers used to address the Almighty in their prayers. The man who began " Paradoxical as it may seem to Thee, O Lord," had no thought of irreverence. Nor had the Aberdeen minister, of whom I have heard, in the beginning of the South African War. He was a stalwart Radical and a great pro-Boer, but he felt himself bound to pray for the success of the British arms, so he prayed as follows: " Bless, O Lord, our soldiers and sailors in South Africa, though, O Lord, as you know fine, it's a question if they've any right to be there." This boldness of speculation is not confined to theology. It has made Scotsmen pioneers in many departments of science and philosophy, as well as in a host of mechanical inventions. Imagination is nothing by itself, but imagination joined to this homely practical standpoint may work wonders. The boldest thinker I ever heard of was an old man who lived at Kirkurd in Tweeddale — he is dead these many years. His hobby was naval and military strategy, and he spent all his time preparing for the defence of Kirkurd against foreign invasion. He used to begin his discourses like this—" Now, supposing there was a Rooshian man-of-war coming up Lyne Water——"

On this commonplace side again, we are thrifty. If you are descended from generations of poor men, you have thrift in your blood. You know that money is hard to come by, and it goes to your heart to see it wasted. But be very careful about the distinction. Scotsmen are not a mean race. There is no man less respected in any Scottish district than a mean man, one who takes mean advantages, who is miserly and crafty and grudging. We hate waste, but upon my soul I think we would rather see a spendthrift than a miser. The Scotsman can be magnificently generous in any cause which touches his heart or his imagination. Look at the private bequests for education; look at the way in which the Free Church at the Disruption raised vast endowments in a year

Some Scottish Characteristics

or two. The Scotsman demands value for his money, but that value may be a spiritual thing, the satisfaction of his conscience, the indulgence of a native kindliness, or the furtherance of some honest ideal. The man who will look at both sides of a shilling for himself may be lavish to his friends. We have never been accused of a lack of hospitality. I remember in South Africa, if you turned up at a Boer farm in the wilds, the farmer would put everything he possessed at your disposal, and treat you like a king. But if it came to buying a horse next morning he would spend hours perjuring his immortal soul over a threepenny bit. There are many features in common between the Boers and the Scots. There is a foolish story which everyone quotes about a Scotsman who complained of the extravagance of London. He said he had not been there an hour when, " bang went saxpence." It is a foolish story, and every Cockney quotes it to illustrate Scots meanness. But they have not got it right. What he really said was, " Bang went saxpence—maistly in wine and cigars." I suspect that the honest fellow was standing treat to his friends.

Some Scottish Characteristics

And last, on the commonplace side of our nature, we are remarkable for our independence. We believe in ourselves. Generations of poverty and struggle have taught us that we must fight our own battles. You remember Sir Walter Scott's words: "I was born a Scotsman and a bare one. Therefore I was born to fight my way in the world, with my left hand, if my right hand failed me, and with my teeth if both were cut off." "Poverty, enterprise, and constant ill-luck," in Stevenson's words, have been the fibre of our national being. No Scotsman at the bottom of his heart has ever much respect for rank, or inherited wealth, or anything except what a man makes for himself. When he goes into the world he is not overburdened with a sense of other people's merits, and he is very confident of his own. Of course, this quality has its unpleasant side. It often leads to needlessly bad manners, and makes him forget that, according to the scriptural promise, it is the meek who shall inherit the earth. Because a man thinks himself as good as his neighbour, there is no reason why he should proclaim it at the top of his voice. It would be well if our countrymen always remembered the real moral of Burns's famous song, "A man's a man for a' that"; for that moral is one of true independence, which is so deep that its possessor does not need to brag about it. There is another point about the quality which I want you to note. A Scot is independent of the world, but he is not independent of his family. Our clannishness is notorious; with us blood is infinitely thicker than water. Indeed, a Scot is independent of the rest of the world largely because he feels that he does not stand alone, but is one of a family, a kinship. We count cousins far afield; and people who to everybody else would be strangers are to us blood relations, bound by the tie of a remote but indissoluble common origin. Things are changing to-day, the family tie is perhaps less close, and in this matter we may be becoming more like our neighbours. But it is not so long ago that over large parts of the Lowlands a wife coming into a family was still called by her maiden surname. She was not *quite* a member of the family, for she had not the claim of blood. I have heard of a Scotsman whose sister went on living with him after his marriage. Somebody pointed out that this was an awkward arrangement for the wife, and he grew very angry. "Do you think," he said, "I wad put away my ain sister for the sake of a strange woman?" And here is a story from the wife's side. Somebody was once condoling with a newly made widow on her husband's death. She dried her tears and consoled herself as follows—" Aweel, aweel. He was a kind man, and he was the faither o' my bairns, but after a' he wasna a drap's-bluid kin to me."

Now I want you to turn to the other side of the Scottish character, the side which is as far distant as possible from the cautious, prosaic, worldly-wise side I have been talking about. With all our prudence, our history is a record of the pursuit of lost causes, unattainable ideals, and impossible loyalties. Look at the long wars of independence which we fought under Bruce and Wallace. If we had had any common sense we would have made peace at the beginning, accepted the English terms, and grown prosperous at the expense of our rich neighbours. Look at the wars of religion, when for a refinement of dogma and a nice point of Church government the best of the Lowland peasantry took to the hills. Look at the Jacobite risings. What earthly sense was in them? Merely because Prince Charlie was a Stewart, and because he was young and gallant, we find sober, middle-aged men, lairds, lawyers, and merchants, risking their necks and their fortunes to help a cause which was doomed from the start. We have, all of us, we Scots, a queer *daftness* in our blood. We may be trusted to be prudent and sensible beyond the average up to a certain point. But there comes a moment when some half-forgotten loyalty is awakened, and then we fling prudence to the winds.

The truth is that we are at bottom the most sentimental and emotional people on earth. We hide it deep down, and we don a mask of gravity and dour caution, but it is there all the time, and all the stronger because we hide it so deep. The ordinary emotional races, like the Latins, are emotional chiefly on the surface. Underneath they are a very mercantile, hard-hearted breed. We are hard on the surface, but few Scotsmen

Some Scottish Characteristics

are not at heart sentimental in the best sense of the word—that is, they can be easily moved by appeals to their generosity or their imagination. You will see that this is true if you consider what type of man the average Scot chiefly admires. Who is the most popular Scottish hero? Not John Knox. Most of us are rather afraid of John, and would shrink from meeting him in the flesh. Sir Walter Scott? Well, I should vote for him personally, because I think he was the finest and wisest type of Scotsman; but if you polled the country you would not get a verdict for Sir Walter. The verdict, I think, would be for Robert Burns. Burns is the man whom most Scotsmen regard with chief sympathy and affection. His words are most often in their memory, not always to their own advantage. And why? Because of the rich humanity, the wild humour, the riotous imagination, the "daftness," in a word, of the greatest of Scottish poets. It is all very strange. If we were the sober, hard-headed, worldly-wise race that our neighbours think we are, we should admire somebody quite different, somebody like Adam Smith. What has such

Some Scottish Characteristics

a race in common with a daft ploughman, whose life was far from respectable, who drank too much, and who lost money in everything he tried? The answer is that we have the main thing in common, for like Burns at bottom we are emotional and imaginative, yes, even the dullest of us. You can test the truth of my view in another way. Scotland has always in political affairs been under the special influence, the spell, of one man. Who is the man who in recent years completely dominated Scotland? There can be only one answer—Mr. Gladstone. And how did he do it? How did he contrive that wonderful Midlothian campaign of 1880, when women brought their little children from far and near to see him, that those children when they grew old might tell of it to their grandchildren? I have lately been turning over some of those Midlothian speeches, and it was not reasoning or argument that played the chief part in their success. It was the prophetic fire of the old man's eloquence, his kindling imagination, the white heat of his moral enthusiasm. In later days Lord Rosebery came very near capturing us, and he worked in the same

Some Scottish Characteristics

way—by appealing to old sentiments of nationality. The moral is that he who would lead Scotland must do it not only by convincing her intellect, but above all by firing her imagination and touching her heart.

Well, on this side of our character, the first and most notable quality is imagination. I need not dwell upon that, but I will give you two illustrations. In the year 1388 or thereabouts, Douglas went raiding into Northumberland, and met the Percy at Otterburne. A great battle was fought in which the Scots were victorious. Percy was captured and Douglas was killed. Now we possess both an English and a Scottish account of the battle. The English ballad is called "Chevy Chase." It tells very vigorously and graphically how the great fight was fought, but it is only a piece of rhymed history. The Scottish ballad of "Otterbourne" is quite different. It is full of wonderful touches of poetry, such as the Douglas's last speech:

> Last night I dream'd a dreary dream
> And I ken the day's thy ain.
> My wound is deep; I fain would sleep;
> Take thou the vanguard of the three,

Some Scottish Characteristics

> And hide me by the braken bush
> That grows on yonder lilye lee.
>
> O bury me by the braken bush,
> Beneath the blooming brier,
> Let never living mortal ken,
> That a kindly Scot lies here.

The two ballads represent two different national temperaments. You cannot get over it by saying that the Scots minstrel was a great poet and the English minstrel a common-place fellow. The minstrels knew their audience and wrote what their audience wanted. The English audience wanted straightforward facts; the Scottish audience wanted the glamour of poetry. The other instance is one which is given by Stevenson. He contrasts the English and the Scottish Catechisms, and he takes the first question in each. The English Catechism begins sensibly and matter-of-factly by asking "What is your name?" Our Shorter Catechism, on the other hand, plunges at once into the deeps of metaphysics and asks "What is man's chief end?" and answers it nobly if obscurely, "To glorify God and to enjoy Him for ever."

A second quality is that curious one

Some Scottish Characteristics

which, for want of a better name, we might call *pride*. It is not the same thing as independence. Independence belongs to our commonplace side; it is a useful business characteristic. Pride is quite useless; it damages a man's career; it prevents him from asking or receiving help; it is self-respect carried to the furthest limits. You have all heard the story of the Highland soldiers who performed some gallant deed, and were summoned to the presence of the King—one of the Georges. They were given each a gift of money, and they thought it due to their dignity, poor men as they were, to distribute this money among the royal servants and porters. The true Scot in adversity will never admit that he is anything but prosperous. He will keep a smiling face when he is starving. He will conceal his misery from the world, and scarcely admit it even to himself. I have heard unfriendly critics of our nation compare us to the Jews; but there is one enormous difference between the two races. The Jew has none of this pride. If he can get on better by making a poor face he will make it. The true Scot is determined to keep a

Some Scottish Characteristics

brave show before his neighbours. He may be beaten, but he is not going to cry out about it.

The third and chief quality of all is our love of adventure. I have explained to you how this arose from our history, and I think it is our most abiding characteristic. We may lose all our other attributes—we may cease to be canny, and drouthy, and God-fearing, but we will always be far-wandering. There is no family in Scotland which has not a number of near relations in the ends of the earth. It is a curious paradox—that the race which is most attached to their homes should be the most eager to travel the world. An American Ambassador in Edinburgh some time ago was explaining how Scotsmen had made the great Republic of the United States. I need not tell you how our people have made the British Empire. Our rule in India was largely due to the young Scotsmen sent out there by Henry Dundas at the time when he was Pitt's right-hand man and the dictator of Scotland. Canada is three-fourths Scottish. There are districts where only Gaelic is spoken, and you will find the same thing, I am told, in

Some Scottish Characteristics

South Australia. In South Africa the occasion when statesmen expound their policy is the St. Andrew's day dinner—a tribute to the preponderating Scottish influence. And wherever you go in the most remote places of the earth you will always find, far away beyond the pale of civilization, a Scotsman, generally making money. We used to be told that when the North Pole was discovered a Scotsman would be found sitting on the top of it. Well, Captain Peary apparently did not find our countryman, and I think that is a very good reason for believing that Captain Peary must have mistaken the place. When the true North Pole is discovered— I believe myself it is somewhere up in the neighbourhood of Carstairs — you will find a Scotsman carrying on a flourishing business beside it. I used to notice in South Africa that when one left the towns and travelled North into the wilds, the signs of civilization gradually got fewer. First the English settlers were left behind, and then the Dutch farmers, until you found nobody but a Jew store-keeper. But if you kept right on, into the heart of savagery, where you thought no white man

Some Scottish Characteristics

had ever been before, you were pretty certain to find a Scotsman.

I remember once when I was young and foolish, I went on a hunting expedition after big game, and we traversed that almost unexplored region, the up-country of Portuguese East Africa. It was a most poisonous place, where white men died like flies, and nothing could live except crocodiles and natives. But right in the heart of it, hundreds of miles from a white neighbour, I found an old Scotsman. He was doing a little gold-mining, and making a fortune by keeping a store for the natives. He was very prosperous and perfectly healthy — I remember yet his wholesome brown face and his clear blue eye. I asked him how he managed to keep alive and well in such a pestilential hole, which everyone believed to be a white man's grave. This was the answer he gave me: " I just keep the fear o' God constantly before my eyes—and drink plenty o' whisky."

I am going to tell you two stories to illustrate our far-wandering character—one absolutely true, the other—well, I won't vouch for the *absolute* truth of the other.

Some Scottish Characteristics

The first is this. About a hundred years ago a German expedition set out to visit the holy cities of the Mohammedan religion, where no infidel is allowed to set foot. It was backed by all kinds of influence, firmans from the Sultan and all the rest of it, and after enormous difficulties and wearful delays it did get to Medina. What was the amazement of the expedition to discover that the governor of Medina, the greatest man in the forbidden city, bore the name of Thomas Keith! It seemed that he had once been a soldier in the Black Watch and had deserted years before. He had found his way to Egypt, where he became a Mohammedan, and by the exercise of Scottish industry and prudence had raised himself in his new faith, till he had become the highest official in the Mohammedan world. That is a pretty outlandish position even for a Scotsman.

But I will tell you a queerer, though I do not guarantee the truth of this second tale. It was told me by a man, who heard it from a man, who had it from the man to whom it happened, and my friend said that to the best of his belief this man

Some Scottish Characteristics

wasn't a bigger liar than the rest of us. The story is this. The narrator, whom we will call Mr. Thomson, was the captain of a Greenock vessel which traded in the East Indian archipelago. On one voyage they encountered a terrific storm, and the ship was driven on the rock-bound coast of one of the islands—I am not sure which—it might have been Borneo, or it might have been New Guinea. The ship went down with all hands, except the captain. He was a very powerful swimmer, and managed to reach a spit of sand, where he lay half-senseless till the morning. When the sun rose and he looked about him, he felt that he was in a pretty bad case. He had no food, and he knew that these islands were inhabited by a peculiarly savage race, who sacrificed all strangers to their gods. He had to face the uncomfortable dilemma of being done to death by savages or perishing of starvation, and he could not make up his mind which was the worse. However, he was saved from the necessity of deciding, for he had hardly taken ten steps from the shore when he was surrounded by a party of armed natives. He expected to be

Some Scottish Characteristics

killed out of hand, but instead, he was conducted through the forest to the chief native city. Here he was given food and lodging and was so well treated that for the moment he began to think that he had fallen among friends. Very soon he was undeceived. One morning he was aroused by a great blowing of shells and beating of drums and a terrific yelling. The streets were crowded with people and he saw that some kind of sacred festival was going on. He was taken out and a wreath of flowers put on his head, while his hands were strapped tightly behind his back. Then he was led through the streets to a great temple which stood on the hill above the city. He realized that it was all up with him, and that he was about to be sacrificed to a heathen god—a miserable fate for a Free Kirk elder in the prime of life. He said his prayers, screwed up his courage, and only hoped that the death would be speedy. Presently he came to the temple, and was led through the great hall into an inner chamber, one end of which was shut off with a huge curtain of skins. His captors prostrated themselves on the ground and rubbed their noses on the floor, and he was compelled to do the same. Then there was another great beating of drums, and to his amazement the natives crawled out backwards, leaving him alone.

Mr. Thomson, I need hardly tell you, was in a miserable state of fright. He was expecting death every moment, but he had no notion what shape it was going to take. There was evidently something behind that curtain, probably a hideous native idol, and any instant priests with knives might appear to take his life. By and by he smelled a curious smell in the place. He could not make it out, but it seemed to him not unlike plug tobacco smoked in a clay pipe. Sure enough he saw little wreaths of smoke issuing from the top of the curtain. Then he saw another thing. There was a hole in the curtain, and out of that hole an eye was looking at him. He was horribly frightened, but he looked again, and then he saw that the eye was a man's eye, that it was a blue eye, and that it was slowly winking at him. Suddenly the curtain was violently disturbed and a voice issued from behind it. And what that voice said was this :—" Godsake, Tammas, is that yoursel' ? How did ye

Some Scottish Characteristics

leave them a' at Maryhill ? " and out from behind the curtain came a big shaggy man with a red beard, decently dressed in a sort of night-gown. The god of the savages turned out to be a Scotsman of the name of Johnston.

Well, these two gentlemen proceeded to hold a sort of "nicht wi' Burns," and Mr. Thomson heard the astounding story of how a Glasgow trader had attained to divinity. It seems that Mr. Johnston had been captured by the natives and very naturally had been condemned to death. But a war was going on with a neighbouring tribe for which every man was required, so he was spared owing to his height and size, and made a captain of the king's body-guard. In the war he greatly distinguished himself, and very soon rose to be commander-in-chief. He was able to show the tribe so many of the ways of civilization, of which they had never heard, that by and by they began to regard him not only with admiration, but with awe. Then a priest raked up an old prophecy about a red god who would come out of the sea and eat up the enemies of the tribe; so after Johnston with some trade dynamite, which he happened to have kept, had blown up the neighbouring capital, he found himself hailed as divine. He saw his chance and took it. As he explained to Mr. Thomson, he had been a good god to those poor, blind, ignorant folk; he had stopped the more horrible of their customs, and he had made them omnipotent in battle. He had also collected a very handsome fortune, chiefly in rubies, and he was now getting ready to go home. The natives were quite prepared for this, for the prophecy had said that the red god would depart in time across the sea. So under his instructions the tribe had built a boat, with which he hoped to reach Singapore. There was only one thing that troubled Mr. Johnston. He was afraid that he had sinned grievously in allowing himself to be the object of heathen worship. " Ye see," he explained, " it's a difficult point. If I have broken anything, it's the spirit and no' the letter of the law. I havena set up a graven image, for ye canna call me a graven image." Mr. Thomson tried to console him by the plea of necessity, and quoted the permission given to Naaman to bow in the house of

Rimmon. But Mr. Johnston was not consoled. " It's no' a case of my bowing in the house of Rimmon. My position is entirely different. Ye see, I'm Rimmon himsel'."

The upshot of the story—which you need not believe unless you like—is that the two of them got safely away and returned to Scotland. Mr. Johnston bought an estate in his native shire, and to salve his conscience he gave largely to Foreign Missions, and built three new, and entirely unnecessary, churches. The last that Mr. Thomson heard of his friend was a letter announcing that he was going to stand for Parliament, and beseeching him never to breathe a word to a soul about his past. " Ye see," ran the letter, " ye cannot expect folk to have any confidence in a man if they kent he had once been a god. Besides, I would never hear the end of it from the hecklers."

Yes, gentlemen, we have the spirit of adventure in our blood, and not only the spirit of adventure, but a power of acclimatizing ourselves, of being at home in strange places. We, the most home-loving race in the world, are yet perfectly happy far away

Some Scottish Characteristics

from home. What is the reason of this paradox? Why does the Scotsman make the best colonist? Why, instead of being home-sick and repining, does he sit down and make a new home for himself, and set about spoiling the Egyptians? I will tell you why. Because centuries of poverty and hard-living have taught him that the true loyalty to Scotland is to do her credit—nay more, that the true Scotland is not the few barren acres of heather he has left, but the Scotland he makes for himself. Scotland is not only the square miles between the Tweed and the Pentland Firth; it is wherever on the face of the earth there are Scotsmen who are true to their faith. The old land indeed remains as a centre of memories and affection; but it is no more the whole of Scotland than Britain is the whole of the British Empire. You will find Scotland among the fisher-folk and the lumber-men of Nova Scotia and Ontario, and among the great cornlands of Western Canada; you will find it in the sheep ranches of Australia, and the farms of New Zealand; in the mines of the Rand, and on the ostrich runs of the Cape. You will find

Some Scottish Characteristics

it in India, and every port of the East; you will find it all over the railways of the world; and on every ship of every flag that carries a Scots engineer. You will hear people talk of the "Scottish nation." Well, I am not sure that we are a nation, for that involves territorial boundaries. We are something greater than that. We are a race. We own no limits of land or water. Scotland is wherever Scotsmen are stamping upon the world the tradition which is our heritage.

I said at the beginning of these remarks that the old Scotland was in many ways fast disappearing. Yes, but there is an imperishable Scotland which can never disappear. We may alter some of our habits, but we will never alter our character. We may change our accent, but we can never change the accent of our mind. Centuries ago there lived a race with which we have many points in common. The Greeks had a small barren country, smaller than ours; therefore they took for their country the whole earth. They carried the Greek tradition far and wide; they were the first pioneers of travel, and the first pioneers of thought; and the civilization they created is still the chief part of our civilization today. We speak of Edinburgh as the "Modern Athens." Well, we are in a sense the modern Greeks, charged like them with a mission and a faith, making our homes over the wide world, and influencing profoundly every society in which we are placed.

I do not think that is too high a claim. To make it good, we must preserve those qualities which have made our race what it is, and chiefly those two great qualities which, as I have been trying to explain, are at the root of the Scottish character. One is that homely grip on fact, that clear-eyed facing of realities, and that intellectual courage which is not dazzled by authority, but claims the right to examine all things. The other is that poetry, imagination, romance—call it what you please—which sees other things in life than material success, and is capable of following whole-heartedly an unprofitable ideal. The first quality alone makes the gross and narrow man of the world; the second alone makes the dreamer and the visionary. The two together produce that most formidable of all combinations, the practical idealist—in other words the true Scot.

Dialect in Literature
By PETER GILES, Litt.D., LL.D.
Master of Emmanuel College, Cambridge.

Delivered at Essex Hall, London, on January 9, 1922.

THE fact that I am speaking under the auspices of this Circle implies that my hearers will be specially interested in dialect as concerned with Scotland. But the problem of dialect is one which is very wide and which has been of importance in other countries besides our own at many periods in the world's history, and therefore you must pardon me if I begin with a more general discussion before I come to consider the question of dialect as it is related to Scotland and to Scottish Literature.

Our subject has all the difficulties that beset the inquirer after truth, and the jesting Pilates of our day might scoffingly inquire, " What is dialect ? " and " What is literature ? " and might not be willing to tarry for the answer. In truth both elements in the problem, dialect and literature, are hard to define, and as regards literature at least, the conclusion might not be satisfactory to all minds ; for, in literature more than in most things, what is one man's meat is another man's poison. The book that in one age is in the hands of every man, in the next age occupies the remotest corner of the library and no man seeks after it.

Dialect in Literature

The question of what is or is not dialect is no less difficult to answer. The word in itself means only a form of speech, but to this has been added in course of time a suggestion that dialect is a form of speech which deviates from a standard. In some countries and in some languages dialect is of much more importance than in others. In modern countries, where the political unit is on so great a scale, it is difficult to realise how important in ancient times, when the political units were small, dialect might be, and how firmly very small communities adhered to the little peculiarities which distinguished them from their nearest neighbours. An area which is full of mountains and rivers, or which consists of small islands, is the kind of area in which dialect is most easily found, has the greatest varieties, and persists the longest. Some years ago an intelligent native of Shetland assured me that he could tell within three miles where any native Shetlander came from. In ancient Greece, where almost every town formed a political unity independent of its neighbour, dialect differences were very numerous and carefully cherished. The most famous of all these communities was Athens; but, great as its fame has been throughout the ages, it was the centre of a political area which was in size somewhat more than twice the dimensions of Kincardineshire, or somewhat less than half the area of Aberdeenshire. Over the mountain from it, as it might be into Banffshire, there lay the country of Bœotia, with a dialect so different that the pronunciation of the Bœotians and their vocabulary were favourite subjects of jesting with the comic poets of Athens. Northwards and westwards from Bœotia lay other districts with dialects probably equally unintelligible to both the Bœotians and the Athenians. But so long as the Greek communities remained independent they each cherished their own peculiarities, and would have resented any attempt to establish a standard to which they should conform outside their own dialect. In that dialect they wrote the inscriptions on their tombstones and their laws, luckily briefer than those of modern states, which, from the imperishable nature of the material on which they were inscribed, remain to us in great numbers to the

Dialect in Literature

present day. It may be said with truth that of most Greek dialects we have really more accurate records than we have of the dialects of our own island. But their gravestones and their laws were intended for the information of their own people. If they wished to appeal to a larger audience, in other words, when they passed from business to literature, they made curious distinctions to which we have no precise parallel. They took a great master of literature as their standard for each particular style, and all later writers in that style had to conform to that standard. If a poet was moved to write a narrative poem of heroes and of battlefields, then he must conform as best he could to the style and language of Homer. If he wished to write a didactic poem on some instructive subject like hunting or fishing, he must follow the form and language of Hesiod, who in his " Works and Days " had first written a poem of the kind. The Greeks had no sporting papers, but their enthusiasm for a successful athlete was no less than our own, and it was a well-paid function of many distinguished poets to hymn the praises of a successful boxer or a charioteer, a wrestler or a runner. The first poet who had written poems of this kind was Stesichorus of Himera in Sicily, and to his style and language the greater poets, whose works to some extent still remain to us, Pindar, Simonides, and Bacchylides, had to conform, although Stesichorus was a Dorian and wrote in the Doric dialect, and Pindar was a Theban, whose language was as unlike that of Stesichorus as could well be, except that the native dialect of Simonides was even farther apart from that of Stesichorus. The language of Attic tragedy, the brilliant compositions of Aeschylus, Sophocles and Euripides were certainly not written in the everyday language of their native town of Athens, though what the history of the tragic dialect may be has not been clearly ascertained by scholars. The same is also true to a considerable extent of prose; nay, it even went so far as doctors' prescriptions, which were written to the best of their ability by Greek medical men in the Ionic dialect of the earliest scientific physicians, just as our own medical men continue to write to-day in a language that by courtesy is called Latin. To these curious practices

Dialect in Literature

we have no parallel. The sporting chronicler, whose picturesque language is a lineal descendant of the vivid metaphors of Pindar, has no special English dialect into which, by tradition, he must convert his glowing periods. It is not necessary for anyone who writes a love-song to fashion it in the metres and the dialect of Burns, as in Greek such a poet had to follow the tradition of Alcaeus and Sappho. Historians like Clarendon and Froude were not bound to conform to the style and language of Holinshed. What Greek authorities would have done with an author like Carlyle is difficult to say; they probably would have cast him into outer darkness. No doubt these curious traditions must have given a certain conventionality to the language of such Greek writers as were bound to compose in a dialect which was not their own, and that may be the reason why later generations found so many of them uninteresting, and did not perpetuate them for our benefit by copying them in later times.

With the disappearance of political freedom the dialects also disappeared. When Greece came under the iron heel of Philip

Dialect in Literature

of Macedon, and still more of his son, Alexander the Great, there was no motive any longer to perpetuate the little local peculiarities. The Macedonians adopted as far as they could the dialect of Athens as their standard, and to this standard in course of time all Greek communities more or less conformed, so that a new " common " dialect, as it was called, was established which was intelligible over the whole of the Greek world, and in which some famous books have been written. Of these the most important is the Greek Testament, which represents the less literary form of this new dialect in a manner closely resembling the language of the documents which in the last thirty years have been dug up in such innumerable thousands from the rubbish heaps of ancient Egypt.

I have dwelt thus long upon these Greek peculiarities because, as I shall show you, we have had something similar in our own country, though we have never utilized forms of language precisely in the same way as the Greeks did. In Latin there is nothing at all like this. Latin, in truth, is but the language of a single town, the dialect of

Dialect in Literature

which was curiously different from almost all its neighbours. From this single town of Rome proceeded by degrees the conquest of Italy and ultimately the conquest of the then known world. There was therefore in Latin always a standard, the standard of the city of Rome, and the scanty fragments of the other dialects of ancient Italy which still survive are very unlike even the earliest Latin, and, in fact, are no closer to Latin than Welsh to Scotch Gaelic. In Greece, at the beginning, every community was a standard for itself; after Alexander's time a new dialect closely modelled on the language of Athens was the standard. For Latin throughout history there was a standard, and but one, the standard of Rome. True, even in Rome itself there were differences. The population of Rome, besides the aristocratic Romans of whom we hear in history and literature, included many traders and other humble folk who spoke a less refined dialect, and a large number of Greek and other foreign slaves whose language, picked up without books, was naturally not more precise than the English of an uneducated negro in the southern states of America.

Dialect in Literature

But of these dialects we learn little from the literature. Ninety-nine hundredths of Roman literature shows no trace of them, but in the history of the languages descended from Latin, French and Spanish, Italian, Rumanian and others, the forms and the vocabulary of these vulgar dialects are of the greatest importance, because language as a whole spreads from the talk of the ordinary man in the street and not from the best writings of the greatest minds.

It is interesting that Latin should have been so uniform, for the geographical configuration of Italy is such as to encourage the formation of dialects. It is divided along nearly its whole length by a range of high mountains which makes a natural separation between the east and the west of the peninsula. In ancient times the mighty river Po divided in two the great plain of the north. The languages, Etruscan and Latin, of the north and south of the Tiber were very different, and there were other natural divisions. In Mediæval and Modern Italy the number of dialects has been very great, and still remains great, though the dialect of Florence has come to be recognized as the

Dialect in Literature

highest type of Italian, because some of the greatest writers of Italy lived and wrote in Florence itself or in its neighbourhood. A country of great plains lends itself less readily to the development of dialect differences because it is more easy for the inhabitants of the different parts of the plain to pass to and fro. In a mountainous country, for some part of the year communication is likely to be impossible, and often for many months together very difficult. Thus it is that in Switzerland are found three main languages, French, German, and Italian, situated respectively on the sides of Switzerland which face France, Germany, and Italy.

But political coercion may compel people of kindred though different languages to think of these ultimately as one and the same. The languages of northern and southern France were really separate languages and not merely dialects, but the result of political union has been to make the language of Paris, the northern capital, the standard for the whole of France, although well into the Middle Ages the south of France had an important literature in Provençal.

Dialect in Literature

In the same way the more mountainous country of Spain, which had, and has, a number of well marked dialects, has been driven by political union to recognize the dialect of Castile as its standard, and to subordinate to it the language of Aragon, which till 400 years ago was an independent country, and that of Catalonia, which is really not Spanish at all, but a language much more closely related to Provençal.

It is remarkable that so many languages have sprung from Latin. Their differences are occasioned partly by the fact that the populations in the different areas spoke languages of different types before they adopted Latin. But that is not the only reason. The differences were also partly occasioned by the different kinds of Latin which they adopted, because Latin did not come into these different countries at the same time. Latin began to conquer Spain from about 200 B.C., but it was not established in Portugal till the reign of Augustus or even later. Provence became romanised before 100 B.C., Northern France was reduced by Julius Cæsar. Rumanian is believed to represent the language of

Dialect in Literature

soldiers settled by Trajan in Rumania about 100 A.D., while between Latin and Italian there has been a gradual development, so that it might be said that there is a greater gulf between classical Latin and Italian than between Spanish or French and classical Latin.

What of dialects in our own country? England like Italy has a backbone extending from the border through Westmorland, Lancashire, and Yorkshire down to Stafford, and continued farther by the Cotswold Hills and the Mendips.

This great ridge, or series of ridges, might be expected to make a marked difference between dialects, and it does; but the most strongly drawn dialect line in England is drawn by the Trent; the dialects north of the Trent and the Humber from Hull to Aberdeen having many features in common which distinguish them from the dialects south of the Trent. The whole history of dialect in this country is conditioned by its original form of settlement and by the invasions of external peoples which have taken place. In Scotland, small as it is, there has been an amalgamation of at least five peoples. In the Lothians were English from a very early period, in Lanark and extending up as far as Dumbarton were the relics of a Welsh Kingdom which had once been continuous across the Solway along the chain of the Pennines to Chester and Wales. But its continuity had been broken by the Saxons at Chester and again at a later period by the Norsemen at the Solway Firth. We are prone to forget in our admiration for the champion of Scotland that William Wallace really meant William the Welshman, and as a native of Lanark a Welshman he naturally was. The form of his name Willelmus Wallensis—in the famous Latin letter sent on the 11th of October, 1297, by Andrew de Moray and Wallace to the authorities of Lubeck and Hamburg—is conclusive enough. An Irish settlement in Argyll grew and multiplied exceedingly and spread across central Scotland, ultimately finding its way to the Firths of Forth and Tay and establishing its language in the ancient kingdom of Fife. In Galloway there was an early population which is described by the chroniclers as Picts, but whether they were of the same stock as the Picts of the north of Scotland

Dialect in Literature

there is hardly evidence to show. The Welsh language of Strathclyde has long disappeared. Of the language of the Scots, which meant originally Irishmen, the Scotch Gaelic is a more broken-down form than its mother language which survives in western Ireland. What the language of the Picts was we hardly know, for their inscriptions, as Andrew Lang said, if correctly transcribed, seem to represent a language which is hardly human. When we talk of Scotch or Scots, we think only of the dialect of English which has gradually spread until it has almost covered the whole land, and yet outside the Lothians, which the English early colonized, it spread but gradually and slowly from little town to little town all along the coast, round the headlands of Fifeshire, and slowly up by the bays of Forfar to Aberdeen and thence to Banff, Cullen, Elgin, and Inverness. To the fourteenth century it was hardly spoken outside the towns; it was the language of traders, and the country inland folk, who won their scanty harvests from alluvial soils along the rivers, spoke only Gaelic. Paradoxical as it may seem, it was Robert the Bruce who was

Dialect in Literature

the chief agent in introducing the English dialect into the north. The hostility of the Earl of Buchan to Bruce's claims had to be avenged when Bruce's star was in the ascendant, and after 1308 Bruce carried fire and sword through the ancient earldom of Buchan, a much larger area than the conventional Buchan of to-day. For fifty years, says Barbour, men " mennyt " (mourned) the harrying of Buchan. From that time onwards the names of the people become English instead of Gaelic, and gradually the understanding of Celtic terms fades away. But it takes long to erase in history "the marks of that which once hath been," and to this day among the older people of Buchan words of the older tongue still survive. A grandchild is still spoken of as an *oy*, and a beetle is still a *goloch*. Just as in England poets may make play with three words for the furze—furze, gorse and whin—so in Aberdeenshire there are three words for the beetle —*beetle*, which is the importation of the Board School; *clock*, which is the old English word found in John Clare's poems from the neighbourhood of Peterborough, as " clock-a-clay" for the ladybird; and *goloch*, which is

Dialect in Literature

the language of the earlier time. Of that earlier language we know a good deal from the names of the natural features of the landscape which are still named in Gaelic, while the farms which in modern times have been recovered from the peat-moss have English names like Whitehill, or Redbog, or Ferniebrae. The numerous names with *auch*-" field," or *tom*-" hill," as Auchnavaird, "the bard's field," or Tombreck, "the spotted hill," because of the many white stones dropped upon it from the ancient icebergs in a prehistoric age, belong to the old Gaelic. Till Gawain Douglas at the beginning of the sixteenth century, no one thought of calling the language anything but English, and the language of the southern kingdom beyond the Tweed was distinguished from it simply as "Southron." The enemies of John Knox, who had lived long in England, and two of whose sons were fellows of St. John's College in Cambridge, charged him with speaking his mother tongue but ill, and Ninian Winzet insultingly said that he would write to him in Latin. "Gif ze throw curiositie of nouationis hes forzet our auld plane Scottis quhilk zour mother lerit zou, in tymes cuming I sall wryte zou my mynd in Latin, for I am nocht acquyntit with zour Southeroun." That was written in 1563, and a little later " Johne Hamilton, student in theologie," in his "Catholik Traictise," makes a similar charge against his adversaries. " Giff king James the fyft war alyue quha hering ane of his subiectis knap suddrone, declarit him ane trateur: quhidder vald he declaire you triple traitoris, quha not onlie knappis suddrone in your negative confession bot also hes causit it be imprentit at London in contempt of our naytive language?" The language of England is merely " southern," the language of Scotland is " Inglis," while the language of the Highlands is described by Dunbar and other poets as Erse, which means Irish, as it originally was. In the earlier period hardly any dialect distinctions for lowland Scotland can be discovered; the language is the same all the way from the Humber to the Moray Firth, but, as time goes on, local peculiarities emerge. The one most characteristic for Aberdeen is the use of *f* for *th* in some words, as in Feersday, earlier Furisday, for Thursday, and in the use of *f* also for *wh* of the ordinary language,

Dialect in Literature

far for *where, funs* for *whins* and so on. This characteristic, which appears also in Ireland, seems to run along the line of junction between the Celtic and the English languages.

So much for the development of dialect. The maintenance and the disappearance, however gradual, of the dialect have next to be considered. The dialect was maintained and fostered by the existence of the northern kingdom, otherwise Scots as a literary medium could have had no more of an existence than the dialects of Yorkshire or of Lancashire; everything would have been absorbed by England much sooner than it has been. The language was the language of the court as well as of the cottar, and James V encouraged it by patronising literary men who could write original works or translate from Latin into the vernacular, the King himself, as one of these transcribers tells us, being " nocht perfyte in Latyne tongue." In Dunbar and in Henryson and others the northern kingdom was fortunate in having writers much superior to any that in England appeared between Chaucer and Spenser. On the other hand the door was opened to the spreading of the southern

Dialect in Literature

dialect by the fact that the Reformation found Scotland without any vernacular version of the Bible. There was indeed a translation made about 1520 attributed to Murdoch Nisbet of Kyle in Ayrshire, but it was entirely unknown to the general public, and is in any case a miserable transliteration of Wyclif's version as amended by John Purvey about 1388. At a time when men were more zealous to search the Scriptures than at any period possibly before or since, it was only natural that the Genevan Version should be in much request in Scotland, and be ousted only by a more perfect form which we know as the Authorised Version. The Reformation had driven the members of the reforming party to take refuge in England, and, like John Knox, many of them no doubt came home again more expert at " knapping Southron " than at pronouncing their mother tongue. When Scotland annexed England at the accession of James to the throne of Elizabeth, and the seat of government was removed from Edinburgh to London, naturally the influence of the southern dialect became, as time passed on, more and more powerful. From the

Dialect in Literature

middle of the eighteenth century this influence became still greater. Allan Ramsay, it is true, put a good face upon it. " The pronunciation," he says, " of Scots is liquid and sonorous and much fuller than the *English,* of which we are masters by being taught it in our schools and daily reading it ; which being added to all our native words of eminent significancie makes our tongue by far the completest : for instance I can say *an empty house, a toom barrel, a boss head,* and *a hollow heart."* Thus, by annexing cheerfully the whole of the English language, he is in this particular instance able to double the vocabulary, for *toom* and *boss* are native, and *empty* and *hollow* in these forms come from the " Southron."

As from the middle of the sixteenth century to the end of the seventeenth the main interest of the common people was centred in theology, and, as no native version of the Scriptures had issued in Scotland from the printing press, the populace were driven from the beginning to use an English version. It is well known what an important element in the warp and woof of the English language and its literature is formed by quotations from the Bible. But it may be doubted whether at any time in the last three centuries the knowledge of the Bible was so general or so thorough in England as it was in Scotland, where not only was it in constant use for devotional purposes as it was in England, but where also the Proverbs formed the commonest of all manuals by which to instruct beginners to read. I am not aware that the history of Scottish school books has ever been thoroughly dealt with, and the subject is one well worth investigation. In this matter Scotland was much more conservative than England and in the middle of the nineteenth century some books were still in use which had first been published in the sixteenth century. When James VI became King of England, Scotland had no intention of ceasing to be a literary centre. But Scottish poets of the end of the fifteenth century and the beginning of the sixteenth century made no appeal to the English reader, because their language was not easily understood and because the fashion of a good deal of the writing of some of them had passed away. Some prose writers, like Pitscottie,

Dialect in Literature

wrote an excellent style, but their circulation in England was again obstructed by the difficulty of their language, and would have been so even if English public interest in Scotland and Scottish affairs had been much greater than it was. From the middle of the seventeenth century onwards, if a Scottish writer desired to make his mark, he must appeal not only to the Scottish but also to the English public. Theological writers had indeed been doing so all along since the Reformation. There was one exception. " Maister Robert Bruce, Minister of Christes Evangel," at Edinburgh, preached in the Scottish dialect and published his sermons, which were so acceptable that they were translated into English and republished in London nearly thirty years afterwards. One quotation from the " Fift Sermon upon the Sacrament " well illustrates this: " It is true and certain that the spunks of faith quhilk are kindled in the heart by the Spirit of God, certain it is, they may be smored for a long time," which is thus rendered in the English version: " It is true and certain, that the sparkles of faith which are kindled in the heart by the Spirit of

Dialect in Literature

God may be obscured and smothered for a long time." But throughout the seventeenth century the Anglicizing tendency in all writings which claimed to be literature was well marked. Yet even in the latter part of the eighteenth century English authorities remarked upon the Scotticisms in the style of such distinguished writers as David Hume and Adam Smith, men who had travelled much and had mixed in the best society. Occasionally Scottish writers still professed that their language was distinct from English. Thus a distinguished lawyer towards the end of the seventeenth century remarks that he thinks " the *English* is fit for Haranguing, the *French* for Complementing, but the *Scots* for Pleading. Our Pronunciation is like ourselves, fiery, abrupt, sprightly, and bold; their (English) greatest Wits being employ'd at Court, have indeed enrich'd very much their language as to Conversation; but all our's, bending themselves to study the Law, the chief Science in Repute with us, hath much smooth'd our Language, as to Pleading." Later the same author says : " Nor can I enough admire, why some of the wanton *English* undervalue

Dialect in Literature

so much our Idiom, since that of our Gentry differs little from their's; nor do our Commons speak so rudely as these of Yorkshire. As to the Words wherein the Difference lies: Our's are for the most part old *French* Words borrow'd during the old League betwixt our Nations, as *cannel* for *cinnamon*, and *servit* for *napkin*, and a Thousand of the like Stamp; and if the *French* Tongue be at least equal to the *English*, I see not why our's should be worse than it. Sometimes also our fiery Temper has made us, for Haste, express several Words into one, as *stour*, for *dust in motion;* *sturdy*, for *an extraordinary giddiness*, etc. Their Language is invented by Courtiers and may be softer, but our's by learn'd Men and Men of Business and so must be more massy and significant: And for our Pronunciation, beside what I said formerly of its being more fitted to the Complexion of our People than the *English* Accent is; I cannot but remember them, that the *Scots* are thought the Nation under Heaven who do with most ease learn to pronounce best the *French*, *Spanish* and other foreign Languages, and all Nations acknowledge that they speak the Latin with the most intelligible Accent; for which no other Reason can be given, but that our Accent is natural and has nothing, at least little, in it that is peculiar. I say not this to asperse the *English*; they are a Nation I honour, but to reprove the Petulancy and Malice of some amongst them, who think they do their Country good Service when they reproach our's."

If it be true that the first petition of a Scot to the Throne of Grace is that he may have a good conceit of himself, we may believe that in this case the prayer had been answered. Of the passage just quoted it might be said in the words of the author, that "it has nothing, at least little, in it that is peculiar." It was written by one of the most famous and the best hated of his countrymen in that day, the famous Sir George Mackenzie, at the door of whose tomb, in the Greyfriars Churchyard at Edinburgh, you may remember Robert Louis Stevenson records that with other little boys he knocked with daring and yet with fear and trembling, while he shouted " Bluidy Mackingie come oot if you da'r," thus perpetuating in the nineteenth century the almost forgotten pronunciation of his name. Yet it was not till the middle of the eighteenth century that the modern pronunciation *Mackenzie* began to oust the correct ancient pronunciation *Mackingie*, and the famous Lord Kames, who still used the Scottish tongue, not only in his social hour, but also on the Bench, declared that the pronunciation of the name as *Mackenzie* turned his stomach. By then the Scottish dialect as a prose medium had practically come to an end. Books in prose, particularly in the folios that our ancestors loved, were very expensive. Scotland was poor, and a book in prose must appeal, if it was to pay, to a larger audience than could be found in Scotland.

With poetry it was different. As we have seen, Allan Ramsay early in the eighteenth century claimed that the Scottish dialect had merits surpassing those of the English, because he incorporated the whole of the English tongue into Scots, and from his day to our own that has been the characteristic of the great mass of Scottish dialect verse which has been written. Ramsay, Fergusson,

Dialect in Literature

Burns, and even in our own day Charles Murray, have never hesitated to eke out the Scottish vocabulary by an English word when it helped the rhyme. This is nothing more than what dialect poets of other languages have also done. Even poetry, if couched in the exact phraseology of the more austere dialects, would have so small a public that one experience of the printer's costs would be sufficient to deter from a second attempt. Yet it is marvellous what a host of little volumes of verse has poured from the Scottish press in the last century and a half. Their writers range through all classes, from Lady Nairne, of an ancient and distinguished family and the ancestress of distinguished members of our present nobility, to tramps and alehouse-keepers. It may be said that generally in this vast mass of literature, mainly second rate or even third or fourth rate, the poems of outstanding merit are those which adhere most closely to the spoken dialect, for the obvious reason that the writer who writes as he thinks and speaks, writes with feeling and conviction. The very success of the distinguished Scottish poets has been the bane of the lesser lights

Dialect in Literature

because, instead of telling their tale in the form in which it framed itself in their thoughts, they must needs cast about to follow in every detail the greater writer whom they imitate. In far the greatest of them all, in Burns himself, it is noticeable that he writes his best when he adheres most closely to his spoken dialect. When he writes in English he is like the stripling David in the armour of Saul, " I cannot go with these, for I have not proved them." The poet, like the painter, must have his eye on the object; if his eye goes straying over the field searching after some great champion, his own execution will not come to much. This is the main reason why for a century the great mass of poetry in the Scottish dialect has been worth so little. Its authors have not dared to be original in form or in subject; instead of being themselves they have been proud to be Burns, it may be, with a touch of Ramsay or Fergusson, or of John Skinner (Tullochgorum), or of the author of Helenore, and a great deal of water. It was remarked by an acute observer that when a great politician died there rarely was a follower ready to succeed him, and

Dialect in Literature

the explanation offered was that great leaders were like mighty forest trees, they overshadowed the young saplings and prevented them from growing. So also it is with the great poets; the striplings catch their accents, they "live in their mild and magnificent eye" and forget that their own proper business is to say their own things in their own way. How many hundreds of Scottish poets have used the "Habbie stanza" because of Ramsay and Fergusson, without any regard to whether it was suited to what they had to say or not?

And what of the future of literature in the Scottish dialect? While Charles Murray and some other minor singers still live, it would be foolish to say that dialect literature is dead, or has no future, but the literature is in some danger of surviving the dialect. There has been a very remarkable change in Scottish dialect within the last generation. If I may trust my ear, the soft, slightly Gaelic accent of Inverness has largely given place to what used to be known as the Aberdeen or Buchan form of the language, and Aberdeen city has appreciably approached nearer to the higher and more nasal notes

Dialect in Literature

of the Glasgow tongue. This must be so, because locomotion is easier than it was, and men move more about the world than they did. Some years ago a benevolent Government was even moved to send an itinerant teacher of English about the Scottish districts to instruct ingenuous youth, a little forgetful perhaps that the children spent at the most five hours in school, and for their other ten waking hours and all their holidays they returned to the language of their parents. But there is no doubt that School Board education has killed many of the old local words. How local these words were, and to some extent still are, can easily be tested by the names of the more technical agricultural implements. How many words are there in different districts for a drill plough ? Some dialect words naturally disappear because times have changed and need for them has ceased. With the disappearance of the box-bed from country cottages has disappeared what seventy or eighty years ago was called a bed-door in Buchan, and a bed-lid in Formartine, only twenty or thirty miles away. According to the old Jacobite song, when George I was called to be our

Dialect in Literature

King he was " sheughin' kail and layin' leeks, without the hose and but the breeks." The word *sheughin'* is a derivative from one of the oldest words in the English language, yet how many are there left in the reign of His Majesty George V who know the word or the employment which it signifies ?

At the beginning I mentioned how the Greek dialects, which had been more numerous and more distinctive in a literary sense than Scottish dialects have ever been, disappeared in the time of Alexander the Great because there was a new literary centre, and also because the men of the mountain valleys of Greece went far afield in the armies of Alexander, and when they came back, if they did come back, had forgotten many of the peculiarities of their ancient tongue. No country sends a larger percentage of its population beyond its borders than Scotland, and even those whose home remains within them often wander afield in a way that was unknown of yore. What of the habits of the northern fishermen fifty years ago and their habits now ? Then, except for a voyage or two before the mast in one of the Aberdeen clippers, they stayed at home, making their

Dialect in Literature

own nets in the winter and weaving their own baskets, and not venturing at that season far to sea; in the summer having a very busy time in the local herring season, but never thinking of following the fish outside their own neighbourhood; for an ordinary catch making a heap of fish for each member of the crew and one for the boat and " casting kavels " to decide who should have which heap; their wives astir in the winter long before dawn to carry to distant homesteads the hard fish which had been carefully cured long before, and returning many weary miles at even with their little bags of oatmeal and potatoes, which kindly housewives had added to the very moderate charges for the fish which by chaffering they had reached. All this is changed and men from Portsoy and Peterhead are more familiar with Lowestoft and Yarmouth than in those days they were with Aberdeen. Naturally such changes of life must bring along with them changes of thought and changes of expression. In time it is probable that our vocabulary will be reduced almost to a dead uniformity, and to return to my previous example, *beetle* will

Dialect in Literature

have replaced not only *clock* and *goloch* in Scotland, but also *straddlebob* and *dumbledore* in England. Even then, however, there will remain some local peculiarities, and if at last the whole population are to speak with one voice, there is at least this comfort, that neither you nor I will be alive to hear it.

The Delight of the Doric in the Diminutive

By J. M. BULLOCH, M.A., LL.D.

Delivered at the Scots Corporation Hall, Crane Court, Fleet Street, London, on December 12, 1921.

WHEN in a passing moment of easy-ozy disregard of my limited learning and leisure, I agreed to address the Vernacular Circle, it was much more than the temptation of alliteration that made me choose for my subject the delight of the Doric in the diminutive: for of all the visions entertained by the vernacularists, the one that has the most solid foundation in actual fact is the persistence in the use of the diminutive, more particularly in the north-east of Scotland, where by far the most vigorous and idiosyncratic form of the vernacular is retained.

Hundreds of mothers throughout Aberdeenshire and Banffshire every night put their " little wee bit loonikies " and " little wee bit lassickies " to their " bedies," while the infant of the household, described as the " little wee eenickie," that is a " teeny weeny eenie " — lies in its " cradlie." A thousand and one examples will leap to your minds :—" The boatie rows " : " sic mannie, sic horsie " ; " the ewie wi' the crookit horn " — as against Burns's " Ca' the ewes tae to the knowes " ; a " sheltie " : a " sheepie," a " lammie," a " burnie," a

The Delight of the Doric

" quinie " and so on through a whole catalogue of diminutives, sometimes five and six thick. Indeed, " a little wee bit loonikie " represents five diminutives. These diminutives are, I say, just as frequently used as ever they have been. They are even employed by people who have sloughed nearly every other vestige of the vernacular, for the very simple reason that they cannot slough the mentality which the diminutive represents and which it can evaluate as nothing else can do.

You cannot go very far into the question of the diminutive in our vernacular without discovering that it is anything but a diminutive subject. To begin with, a full expiscation of the subject, as the creator of Johnny Gibb would have said, would require the knowledge of a comparative philologist, for diminutives are widely used by the Russians, the Dutch, the Germans, especially the south Germans, and the Italians. The Russian diminutive suffix " ka " as in " Petrouchka," is just the Scots " kie " as in " loonikie " : and the German " chen " as in " Mädchen," is our " kin." The Dutchman's " je " or " tje " as in *in the Diminutive*

" Kleintje " a child, is our " ie " as in " bairnie," and so on.

But in addition to the mere philological aspect of the problem, you will find, at any rate in the case of Scotland, many other applications which go deep down into national psychology. The diminutive, in short, is not an isolated phenomenon. It is simply one way, and merely the vocal way, of giving expression to a general method of minimising, which affects mind and matter alike. To begin with the visible world; the cattle of Scotland were once much smaller than they are to-day—infinitely less than the monsters of the modern showyard, and the familiar word " stirkie " still remains to indicate the smaller animal of other days. Then the hardy black-faced sheep on our hills are still on the small side for the very obvious reason that they cannot get the luxurious pasture which increases the size of sheep on the Romney marshes or in Southdowns; and similar reasons dwarf the Shetland pony still more. The people themselves were also much smaller than they are to-day, particularly in the Highlands. Thus the first muster roll of the Gordon

The Delight of the Doric

Highlanders in 1794 showed the average height of the 914 recruits as 5 ft. $5\frac{1}{2}$ in., a fact that made many newspaper correspondents very angry when I stated it a few years ago, though the scientific experts tell us that the short sturdy man makes by far the best soldier, both on physiological and psychological grounds. Of course, the former smallness of the ordinary man is not confined to Scotland: the suits of armour at the Tower remain to demonstrate the same thing on this side of the Border.

But the diminutive remains dominant to this day in the Scots mind, distinguishing it very distinctly from the mind of the pukha English, who use hardly any genuine diminutives of their own. It expresses itself very definitely in the Scot's religion, for Calvinism is based fundamentally on the conception of man as a puny creature struggling with a colossal predestined fate. Although the more literal interpretation of Calvinism has passed away, despite its irresistible logic, the effect of it remains very powerful to this day. How often all of us have heard some such answers as this to our youthful grumbling over a rainy day:—" Be thankfu'

in the Diminutive

ye've a roof ower yer heid ": " Think o' them upon the sea " : or, in other relations ; —" Be thankfu' ye've a hale skin ": or " Be thankfu' for sma' mercies " : and, more general still, " Keep a calm sough." Similarly, when the Scot expresses his emotions in music he uses the curtailed pentatonic, and loves to strike the minor key—note the technical word — with all that wistfulness which made Wordsworth listen wonderingly to the solitary Highland lass " breaking the silence of the seas among the farthest Hebrides." Precisely the same reasons lie at the root of our national tentativeness, our canniness. Outsiders are apt to think we are full of self-assurance. But the very reverse is the case, deep down in us. For if we are tenacious, we are also very tentative, with an ever-present sense of what the pagan calls the sword of Damocles, and the Christian calls the hand of God.

I have been trying to explain to myself for many years the sources of our national mentality on some such lines as these, and I have, consequently, been immensely interested by a corroboration in the parallel case of the Dutch. The people of Holland,

The Delight of the Doric

it appears, are nearly as fond of diminutive suffixes as ourselves. Thus the Dutchman calls his child a " Kleintje," which literally translates into our " littlin." He will speak of his breakfastie, or his dinnerikie. Mr. Brian W. Downs, of Christ's College, Cambridge, the co-author of a new grammar of the Dutch language, published by the Cambridge University Press, in the course of a long and illuminating letter to me, says : — " It may interest you to know that in Dutch a high proportion of diminutives in more or less colloquial use was identified with pietist religion, with the eighteenth century movements which correspond to our Methodism."

I am anxious, however, to go a step beyond Mr. Downs. Why should the people have the diminutizing habit at all ? Not being a philologist, and approaching the subject as the merest amateur, I have canvassed, ever since I was rash enough to promise this paper, a great many different people. I regret to say I have almost wholly failed to pick up an explanation from any of them. Indeed, one man with a very distinguished Oxford career behind

in the Diminutive

him, brushed me aside with the assertion that there is no cause for the use of the diminutive: he contented himself with the facile explanation that it is simply "a fashion." Not having lived so long as he has done away from our intensely rational corner of the country, and regarding facts merely as symbols of something far deeper —though I may not always understand what it is—I simply cannot bring myself to believe that there is no cause for the persistent use of the diminutive. I feel instinctively that there's " aye some watter far the stirkie droons "; only, the difficulty is to find the " watter." I am convinced that the spoken word is merely the mirror of the mind, the surface expression of a mental mood; and, believing that, I never despair of the vernacular, for the mentality of our countrymen has not varied very much, and in any case it is radically different from that of the Englishman. In search (which is surely very Scots) for first causes, I have again been greatly encouraged by Mr. Downs, for he corroborates all I had thought out for myself when he writes me : — " The real cause for the prevalence of diminutives would appear to

The Delight of the Doric

be primarily psychological—though I should think philological reasons might well be contributory." But he adds this :—" About the psychology of speech origins, I do not believe anything reliable is known." I am therefore left alone to develop my own theory of the basis of that psychology.

The mentality of a people is largely conditioned by the character of the climate they live in, and the climate is in turn conditioned by latitude, so that you are quickly immersed in a physiographical investigation on which I am quite incompetent to enter. I have long felt, to take one poignant example, that the climate of Ireland is the main cause of the curious temper of the people —Sinn Fein, Nationalist, and Loyalist alike : otherwise I do not understand why an Irish terrier is so pugnacious, and why an Irish hunter has so much spirit. Though this aspect of climatology is in its veriest infancy, it has long been vaguely apprehended, just as heredity was believed in, thousands of years before Darwin made a doctrine of it. It stands out clearly for instance in the bull of Pope Alexander VI, who, in founding the University of Aberdeen in 1494, attri-

in the Diminutive

buted the "rude and ignorant" character of the people, especially in the Highlands, to the fact that they were cut off from the rest of the kingdom by "firths and very lofty mountains"—"*per maris bracchia et montes altissimos*" are his actual words. Consider for a moment the geographical position of Aberdeenshire, to take one of the group under discussion. It stands on a huge out-thrust of granite, so hard that the sea has been unable to wash it away—especially in the Buchan district, where the diminutive is very strong — as it has gouged out the soft Kincardineshire coast and still more so further south. On the east and north, the natives of the shire had to face this particularly bleak stretch of sea. On the north and west, they felt dwarfed by the Grampians and Cairngorms, while the people living in, rather than on, the intractable land between these formidable forces were literally between the devil and the deep sea. In consequence, they developed a distinct type of character, and, as they were cut off from the rest of the country, and as they have always to keep the forces that tend to non-cultivation at bay, they retain those characteristics long after the original climatic conditions have been considerably modified by their industry and the knowledge, created largely by the University, which has had an enormous effect on its whole hinterland, even among people who have never crossed its hospitable threshold. At first, however, the mere human element, as you can well understand, was completely midgeted by the vast physical forces of nature around it. Obviously it made for poor crops and therefore inadequate food, just as the scanty hill herbage makes for little sheepies. And on the spiritual side it made man feel a very small creature indeed, in the face of the tremendous physical odds against him, odds that primitive people are wont to anthropomorphise into all sorts of vengeful deities.

I fancy that it is their conflict with the perilous sea that makes northern fisher folk so keen on the use of diminutives, especially in the matter of tee-names. I remember once seeing a gigantic fisherman who was known as " Johnikie's Willikie." That was the name he had got in childhood, and it stuck to him as an indispensable distin-

in the Diminutive

guishing mark throughout life. His father in childhood had probably been called Johnikie, and when he had a son William, the child was called Willikie, but in order to distinguish him from other Williams in the village he would be called Johnikie's Willikie. The vernacular of our fisherfolk, however, is a thing apart and cannot be entered on here, although it is a very fascinating subject.

I do not suggest that my theory with regard to the diminutive in our Doric can be applied as a universal generalization. For example, it will hardly explain why the diminutive is common in late Latin, and in Italian, but not in French: though I can well understand why a country like Switzerland with its overmastering mountains and precarious valleys should have produced Calvin and his creed—a creed which you can never associate with the happier climes of the Latin, who contemplates his vineyards and olive groves almost automatically cultivated by the sun. On the other hand, you can easily understand how the Russian, midgeted by his immense steppes, and his formidable winters, should dote on

The Delight of the Doric

the diminutive, as when he speaks of his country as " Matushka "—that is simply " Mitherikie," and of the Tsar as " Batouska," which the Englishman translates as " Little Father," whereas the Scot with his love of diminutives would render it " Fatherikie." This Russian analogy lends some support to Sir Arthur Keith's theory that Aberdeenshire was at one time inhabited by a people not unlike the Wends, who are largely Slavonic.

While the men of science are shy of venturing on a physiological explanation of the differences of language and dialect, the more imaginative Maurice Hewlett once suggested that " climate has much to answer for in the growth of language," citing the various transformations of the same word in different languages. Though he did not do so, he might very well have cited Grimm's familiar law, with such a word as the Latin " pater " becoming " père " in French, " padre " in Italian, " vater " in German, " father " in English, " fader " in some parts of Scotland. Whether it was the " climate or some palatal formation of the indigenes " which is responsible for such transforma-

in the Diminutive

tions, Mr. Hewlett felt that he was "not scholar enough to say." May we not suggest, however, that the "palatal formation" is caused by the climate and the geography of a place, which seems to affect some bone structures, and is certainly the cause of certain diseases like that form of home-grown "goitre" to which we give the name of Derbyshire neck ?

You may think I'm "haverin'"; that my theories are very much up in the air. But we come down to acknowledged *terra firma* in considering the main use to which the diminutive is put, and why it has become quite indispensable as an instrument of expression. Curiously enough it is used to express two diametrically opposite emotions —Affection and Contempt—in which we as a people, who understand white and black —whereas the Englishman can see the whole spectrum at once—are particularly strong.

It is very easy to see how the diminutive described at once the physical smallness of a child, and the affection created by the child. In relation to this fact I have heard Dr. Fleming describe an Aberdeenshire family. The landowner was called the "laird";

The Delight of the Doric

his son, the heir-apparent, was called the "lairdie," and the latter's son was known as the "lairdikie." Scots nursery rhymes can well claim to be infinitely more true and tender than English ones; because, in addition to the diminutive, the Doric has the further advantage of eliminating consonants, and cultivating vowel sounds, as in the phrase, " a' ae oo," which saves it from being babyish, or mawkish. A good example of the vowel sound is the use of the word " doo-ie," that is, a young " doo," or dove. I have heard of a Portsoy mother who used to describe her progeny as " the dooie Annie; the infant Thedor; the rascal Rob; and the loon Jock."

For nursery rhymes the diminutive is unsurpassable for its sense of tender perception of the fascinating helplessness of the object addressed. Take for instance :

> Dance to your daddie,
> My bonnie laddie.
> Dance to your daddie, my bonnie lamb !
> And ye'll get a fishie
> In a little dishie—
> Ye'll get a fishie when the boat comes hame.

in the Diminutive

> Dance to your daddie,
> My bonnie laddie,
> Dance to your daddie, my bonnie lamb!
> And ye'll get a coatie,
> And a pair o' breekies—
> You'll get a whippie and a soople tam.

That jingle was given in " Chambers' Popular Rhymes of Scotland " more than seventy years ago, but the same sort of thing is being said and sung to-day. Take for example Mr. John Mitchell's delightful " crack " with his little grandson:

I hae a wee man that I ca' Donal' Dhu,
Wi' rosy red cheekies an' een o' deep blue.
A sweet dimpl't chin an' a cherry ripe mou,
O a bonnie wee mannie is my Donal' Dhu.

Wi' a towie bit powie o' flaxeny hue,
An' his pink tippet luggies aye bo-peepin' throo
The curlies that dance roon his lily fite broo,
O a cantie wee carlie is my Donal' Dhu.

His chubby bit nievie he pokes in my mou,
He steeks baith my een, an' my nose he will pu'.
Syne lauchs in my face an' says "gooie goo goo,"
O a trickie wee nickum is my Donal' Dhu.

Note how the diminutive is applied not merely to the child itself, but to the different parts of his anatomy, as in the rhyme:—

The Delight of the Doric

> Hap an' row, hap an' row
> Hap an' row the feeties o't;
> I never kent I wis a dad
> Until I heard the greetin' o't.

It is even applied to wholly inanimate objects. "Come under my plaidie" leaps at you as a lover's litany before you have any dealings with the nominative addressed "dear lassie." Note the lines:

At nicht when the wee thing had suppit her parritch I washed wi' a will her bit duddies mysel.

"Duddies" connotes a world of tender pathos, very difficult to express in any didactic phrase in cold English.

I may note in passing that in many parts of Scotland the diminutive if used at all, takes the form of an adjectival affix like "wee," whereas people in the north adopt a suffix which forms one word. The Glasgow people say "wee yin," now combined into "wean," whereas the northerner would say "een-ie," or "eenickie."

It need hardly be said that the diminutive is used extensively, especially in verse, to express affection for grown-ups, and forms the very foundation of the love lyric throughout Scotland generally. Burns simply teems with it. I have been fortunate to get an extremely interesting expression of opinion on this aspect of the question from Miss Mary Symon of Dufftown, the author of the moving poems on " Neuve Chapelle," and " The Soldier's Cairn." Miss Symon is not only a constructive artist of a very high quality, but she is an extraordinarily incisive critic of our psychology, and a past master of our most distinctive Doric, and of all the people I have canvassed she has flashed by far the most brilliant beam of understanding. She sums our way of expressing emotion in these words :—

Diminutives are our only emotional outlets. We have practically no endearments. The southerner spreads himself out on " dears," " darlings," " beloveds " and such-like saccharinities. The tidal wave of passion swamps the Scot. Even the mildest of ordinary, everyday loves remain unexpressed either directly or indirectly because there is no vocabulary for them. It is somebody of Barrie's, I think, who says : " Love ye ? Weesht ! Fat kin' o' a word's that to be makin' eese o'—an' fowk a' weel eneuch." In a vague unformulated fashion we consider tenderness a weakness, very nearly an

The Delight of the Doric

indecency. At any rate we fight shy of it. We *are* shy of it. " Love, but dinna lat on " about sums up all the erotic philosophy of the hill plaid and the sleeved weskit. So in our soft moments—no dithyrambics, no little urbanities, or amiabilities. We just drop into diminutives.

The diminutive is also unmatchable in expressing humour. The locus classicus of this use of it is the delicious story of the " Wee bit Wifeikie." This ditty is usually attributed to " the well-known priest, Alexander Geddes, but the author of " The Bards of Bon Accord " has recently decided that it is the work of an Aberdonian, Alexander Watson, who died in 1831 at the age of 87. Mr. Walker quotes from Watson's manuscript at the British Museum, which leads me to note in passing that the great bulk of northeastern verse was printed in a conventional form, and does not represent the actual pronunciation of the writer or the reader. I am certain, for instance, that whether Watson or Geddes wrote the " Wee Wifeikie," neither of them ever used the word " frae " for " from," though the British Museum manuscript actually does so.

Let me say in parenthesis that one of

in the Diminutive

the earliest printed examples of the use of the diminutive occurs in Alexander Barclay's curious book "The Calendar of Shyppars," that is Shepherds, which was first printed in Paris in 1503. Barclay, who belonged to the north of Scotland, seems to have written Scots in a phonetic way, which Mr. Kellas Johnstone has most laboriously construed. It will be found that he often used diminutives, notably "parties" for parts.

Humour links up the third great use of the diminutive as an expression of contempt, and so far as I can gather our Doric is peculiar in using it for this purpose. It is, however, not difficult to understand how affection runs into humour, or rather wit, and then into contempt. We are constantly told that the Scot has no humour. What the Scot has got is wit, a very different quality. Humour is a quality of the heart: wit is the product of the head. It is not because the Scot has no heart. The trouble is he feels that he has too much of it. Thus he instinctively sets his head to sentinel his heart, so that he may not go off at the deep end of rapturous enthusiasm or display too much affection. He, therefore, camouflages his

The Delight of the Doric

feelings, his prejudices, by an air of great judicialness, " a rather awful kind of levelheadness " as Mr. Galsworthy once called it in speaking of the Englishman. He becomes almost the *advocatus diaboli,* and in that mood he can develop a withering, devastating, desiccating analysis which goes through your very marrow. This is the "acid test" to the nth degree of acidity. All of us have known and suffered from this type of our countrymen, and in consequence our heads, in Henley's phrase, have been bloody—but I hope not bowed.

Now there is nothing like the diminutive for expressing this mood, for, just as the diminutive is admirable for expressing the physical smallness of a child, and the child quality in the things we love, so it represents equally well all kinds of spiritual smallness and meanness.

Not the least curious feature of this is the way in which this use of the diminutive tempts a man to give his real estimate of his fellows. The canniest man I know, a Scots lawyer, who never can be induced to express a strong opinion about anybody, involuntarily lets himself go by using the

in the Diminutive

diminutive. He always speaks of a " covie " or " mannie " in describing a certain " sanshach " type of character. In this respect the diminutive does for the Scot what the understatement does for the Englishman. The creed of the understatement is summed up for the well-bred Englishman by the typical Tennysonianism—" Be not the first and not the last " ; and for the Cockney by such phrases as " Not 'alf " and " I don't think." But the Scot, knowing little of compromise, can go the whole hog of criticism. Here is a typical example. I was once driving through a certain parish in Aberdeenshire when the coachman, on being asked who lived in a particular mansion off the road, described the " laird " as a " wiffer waffer o' a cratur." " What's that ? " asked one of the party, who was innocent of the vernacular. " A damned naething ava'," was the prompt reply, and as a matter of fact it was an incisively accurate description of the occupant, a fussy and peppery colonel of the old " Nabob " type.

Touching the word " wiffer waffer," you will note that we have a great many words not strictly diminutive so far as I know

The Delight of the Doric

which express littleness of some kind or other—thus " shargar " for a physical dwarf, " ablach " (a pure Gaelic word) for an insignificant person mentally and physically, or " foumart " which really means a pole cat.

Just as the affectionate use of the diminutive has its locus classicus in the " Wee bit Wifeikie," so the contemptuous use of the process has its classic expression in Wee German lairdie :—

> Wha the de'il ha'e we gotten for a king
> But a wee, wee German lairdie ?
> And, when we gaed to bring him hame,
> He was delving in his yairdie ;
> Sheughing kail, and laying leeks,
> But the hose, and but the breeks ;
> Up his beggar duds he cleeks—
> This wee, wee German lairdie.

I have said that the use of the diminutive is most prevalent in the north-east of Scotland, particularly in Aberdeenshire and Banffshire, but it is also used in Kincardineshire, Forfarshire, and Fifeshire, and as far north as Ross-shire, which seems to corroborate Mr. Kellas Johnstone's belief that the Aberdeenshire dialect is creeping down and up the coast. In illustration of this,

in the Diminutive

a Forfar friend cites " a little wee bit gniff gnaff o' a doggikie "; while a Ross-shire newspaper recently printed a set of verses by Donald A. Mackenzie entitled " Granny's Baking," described as being " in Cromarty dialect." It begins thus:

When grannie bakes her oaten cakes,
   I aye drap in to news a whiley—
If she should want a messagie,
   She'll ken that then I'd run a miley.
My grannie's cakes are groff and sweet—
   She'll aye mak ane for her " wee mannie ":
On east or west in Cromarty
   There's none can bake like my auld grannie.

She'll say: " Noo tak' the pailie doon
   And get a Stroopie drink for grannie:
Ye'll mind and row yer hankie roon
   The han'lie or 't'ill hurt yer han'ie."—
In comes the weaver's wife to crack
   Wi'—" Bless yer he'rt and hoo's yer body? "
I ken my cakie's toastin' fine,
   As I go up the Stroopie roadie.

Nobody would claim this as great poetry, but it has the " charrum," as Maggie Wylie would say, of being couthie, and it is quite typical of much that is being spoken in the

The Delight of the Doric

north-east of Scotland to-day. This is so much the case that you will find the diminutive rarely printed. It is so natural, so much part of the common coinage that Scots "makars," either of yesterday or of to-day, rarely employ it. They think it too common, too colloquial, not "literary" enough. That is really one of our cruxes. The moment the Scot begins to write, he tends to become self-conscious, not least when he writes in English, because he does not write as he speaks, whereas the Englishman does. Even in Scots, a poetic convention tends to set itself up in print.

It is this more than anything that induces some critics of the Vernacular Circle, especially in Scotland, to regard us as so many Burkes and Hares, resurrecting the bones of a dead language. So vital a thing as our vernacular cannot die. Let it be freely admitted that it undergoes change precisely because it is alive; for, as Ibsen once said, the only thing that doesn't change is the law of change. True, the auld hoose of our Doric—which has extended beyond the old but and ben, tends to get out of the plumb, and the proud task of the Vernacular Circle is to do a bit

in the Diminutive

of underpinning, mostly, however, by inducing our stay-at-home compatriots to write it as they speak it, for it shows far fewer cracks when it is spoken colloquially.

Certain it is, the diminutive changes least of all, because it expresses as nothing else can do the most marked characteristics of our mentality. Why, indeed, should the Scot abjure his thriftiness and cripple his vocabulary by casting aside an instrument of expression which saves the inspiration of his childhood from fading into the light of common day: an instrument so gracious, so expressive, so tender, so humorous; instinct with an element of that criticism of life which Matthew Arnold defined as the essence of poetry. The diminutive in our vivid vernacular makes all of us poets *in posse*, whether we know it or not, and the spirit of poetry, more than anything else, gives us greater power to face the prose of a work-a-day world and has made Scotsmen what they are.